UNDERSTANDING THE JOURNEY FROM SELF-DEFEATING BEHAVIOR TO SELF-LOVE

Nurturing Your Spirit, Cultivating Your Worth, and Becoming Your Best Self!

By: Jenifer Taylor

Text Copyright 2024 – © Jenifer Taylor.
All rights reserved worldwide. No part of this publication may be republished in any form or by any means, including photocopying, scanning, or otherwise, without prior written permission from the author.

TABLE OF CONTENT

INTRODUCTION — 8

CHAPTER 1: UNDERSTANDING SELF-DEFEATING BEHAVIORS — 10

How the Brain Interprets Self-Defeating Behaviors — 11

Neuroplasticity and Changing Behaviors — 13

Practical Techniques for Rewiring the Brain — 14

Steps to Change Self-Defeating Behaviors — 15

What is Self-Love? — 16

Self-Love vs. Self-Care — 16

The Role of Self-Compassion — 17

Strategies to Cultivate Self-Compassion — 18

Cultivating an Authentic Self-Identity — 19

Steps to Discover Your True Self — 19

Implementing Self-Love Daily — 22

Daily Self-Love in Action — 24

CHAPTER 2: UNRAVELING THE MYTHS — 25

ADDRESSING COMMON MYTHS — 25

The Truth Behind Self-Love — 28

The Science and Psychological Benefits of Self-Love — 28

Embracing Diversity in Self-Love	29
Cultural Perspectives on Self-Love	29
Age and Life Stages	30
Gender and Sexual Identity	31
Socioeconomic Factors	32

CHAPTER 3: THE PSYCHOLOGICAL FOUNDATIONS OF SELF-LOVE — 34

Simplifying Complex Research	34
The Role of Self-Love in Personal Development	35
Self-love and Mental Health	37
Practical Advice for Enhancing Mental Health Through Self-Love	38
Overcoming Negative Self-Talk	39
Building Emotional Resilience	42
Cultivating Resilience Through Self-Love	42
Connecting Happiness and Self-Love	44

CHAPTER 4: CHILDHOOD AND ITS LASTING EFFECTS — 45

How Early Experiences Influence Adult Behavior	45
Reflection Prompts to Uncover Early Influences	48
Navigating the Impact of Childhood on Self-Love	49
The Role of Parenting Styles	50
How Parenting Styles Affect You	51

Healing and Moving Forward	51
Healing from Childhood Trauma	53
Therapeutic Approaches to Healing	53
Re-parenting Yourself: Nurturing Your Inner Child	55
The Power of Forgiveness: Embracing Self-Love Through Letting Go	58
Forgiveness as a Path to Healing	60

CHAPTER 5: THE RELATIONSHIP BETWEEN SELF-LOVE AND BODY IMAGE — 61

Challenging Societal Standards	61
Embracing Body Diversity and Inclusivity	62
Journey to Self-Acceptance: Embracing Your Body	65
Strategies to Cultivate Body Acceptance	65
Overcoming Body Shame: Embracing Self-Compassion and Confidence	67
Celebrating Your Body: Learning to Appreciate Your Physical Self	69

CHAPTER 6: SELF-LOVE IN RELATIONSHIPS — 71

The Foundation of Mutual Respect	71
Setting Healthy Boundaries: Essential Strategies for Personal Well-Being	72
How to Identify Your Personal Boundaries	74
Tips for Maintaining Boundaries	76
Exiting Toxic Relationships: Embracing Freedom and Self-Respect	78
Steps to Safely Exit Toxic Relationships	78

Prioritizing Self-Love: Foundation for Healthy Relationships — 81

CHAPTER 7: SELF-LOVE AND CAREER SUCCESS — 88

Aligning Work with Self-Worth — 88

Combating Impostor Syndrome — 91

The Power of "Saying No": Empowerment through Selective Commitment — 95

Finding Work-Life Balance: Harmonizing Professional Goals and Personal Well-being — 98

Recognizing Your Achievements: Celebrating Your Successes — 102

Strategies to Acknowledge Your Accomplishments — 103

CHAPTER 8: PRACTICAL STEPS TO CULTIVATE SELF-LOVE — 105

Mindfulness and Self-Love: Cultivating Presence and Compassion — 113

Types of Mindfulness Practices — 113

Creating a Self-Love Ritual Using Mindfulness — 114

Affirmations for Confidence: Enhancing Self-Esteem Through Positive Statements — 115

How to Craft Effective Affirmations — 115

Journaling for Self-Discovery: Unlocking Inner Wisdom — 117

Integrating Journaling into Your Self-Love Practice — 118

CHAPTER 9: OVERCOMING OBSTACLES TO SELF-LOVE — 120

Identifying Blockers: Techniques for Recognizing and Addressing Self-Love Obstacles — 120

Handling Setbacks: Sustaining Self-Love Through Challenges	122
Strategies for Maintaining Self-Love Through Challenges	123
Dealing with Loneliness: Embracing Solitude and Cultivating Self-Compassion	125
Balancing Expectations: Staying True to Yourself Amid External Pressures	128
Embracing Vulnerability: Discovering Strength in Openness	130
Common Situations of Vulnerability	130

CHAPTER 10: LIVING A LIFE FUELED BY SELF-LOVE — 133

Making Self-Love-Driven Decisions	133
Extending Love to the Community: Enhancing Well-being Through Shared Compassion	135
How to Share Love in the Community	135
Benefits of Community Engagement	136
Real-Life Examples	136

POSTPARTUM DEPRESSION AND SELF-LOVE — 138

Types and Symptoms of Postpartum Depression	138
Signs and Features to Look Out For	139
Practical Strategies to Assist You	140

Introduction

> "I can be changed by what happens to me. But I refuse to be reduced by it." – Maya Angelou.

Imagine a life where you truly embrace and love yourself, regardless of the challenges you face. What would change? How would you feel? Resilience is the key to this transformation. It's the strength that allows you to rise from the ashes of adversity, turning challenges into stepping stones.

Standing at the crossroads of life, the path less traveled often leads to the deepest and most profound destinations. For me, that path was one of self-love and healing. My journey began in the shadows of an oppressive and abusive marriage, a place where I felt more like a prisoner than a partner. Have you ever felt trapped, not just by physical walls but by the barriers within your own mind? That was where I found myself—confined by fear and diminished by doubt.

I remember that very moment when the weight of staying became more daunting than the fear of leaving. It was a cold morning, the kind where your breath turns to mist before your eyes, and I decided that I would rather brave the unknown than endure the unbearable. That decision was my first act of self-love. It wasn't just about leaving a place; it was about leaving behind an identity that was no longer mine and stepping towards a self that needed to be rediscovered and cherished.

- What fears are holding you back from making a choice that could liberate you?
- How might your life change if you embraced yourself fully and without reservation?

As I navigated through the challenges of single motherhood and the complexities of starting over in a new country, each step forward was fueled by an emerging sense of self-worth and the relentless pursuit of personal peace. This journey was not just about healing from past wounds—it was about building a new foundation on which I could grow, flourish, and empower others.

Why Does this Story Matter?

In sharing my story, I want you to look within and recognize your own capacity for transformation. Self-love is not a luxury but a necessity, vital for anyone wishing to lead a fulfilled and authentic life. Your relationship with yourself is the most essential one you will ever have.

- Why do we often struggle to grant ourselves the compassion we readily offer to others?

- What might change in your life if you treated yourself with the same kindness and understanding you provided to your friends and family?

This narrative is about your growth, strength, and wisdom. It spans personal, professional, and spiritual aspects, highlighting the transformative power of self-love in your life.

As you engage with these insights, I encourage you to read, reflect, question, and challenge yourself. Use the lessons and perspectives shared in this book as tools to nurture your own journey. Think about the changes you want to make in your life and take that first step toward treating yourself with more love, self-compassion and respect.

Happy reading!

Chapter 1: Understanding Self-Defeating Behaviors

"Loving yourself isn't vanity. It is sanity." – Katrina Mayer.

Before we can fully embrace the richness of self-love, we must first confront the barriers we often unwittingly construct against it. These barriers, known as self-defeating behaviors, are the habits and thought patterns that prevent us from achieving our full potential.

What are Self-Defeating Behaviors?

Self-defeating behaviors are actions or thoughts that keep you from nurturing your own growth and happiness. They can manifest as *procrastination, self-doubt, perfectionism,* or even as destructive habit of comparing yourself to others. Have you ever set a goal, only to find yourself sabotaging it through procrastination or setting impossibly high standards? That's self-defeating behavior at play.

To change these patterns, we first need to understand their roots. Often, they stem from our past experiences—perhaps criticism we received in childhood or unrealistic expectations placed on us by others. These experiences can seed doubt in our capabilities and worth, which grows into self-defeating behavior as we carry these beliefs into adulthood.

Think of a child who often heard criticisms like, "You're not smart enough," or "You'll never succeed." As this child grows into adulthood, they might hesitate to pursue new opportunities or challenges, fearing that they will inevitably fail. This fear of failure, deeply ingrained from repeated negative feedback, can lead to a cycle of avoiding risks and settling for less, reinforcing the belief that success is out of reach.

Self-Defeating Patterns

Identifying these behaviors in yourself can be challenging because they often form part of our subconscious routine. To start, it's helpful to reflect on areas of your life where you feel stuck or unsatisfied. Ask yourself:

- **What negative thoughts recur in these situations?** Think about moments when you feel overwhelmed or anxious. Do you find yourself thinking, "I can't do this," or "I'm not good enough"? These recurring thoughts can be indicators of deeper self-defeating patterns.

- **Are there patterns of behavior that seem to sabotage your happiness or success?** Look at instances where you've set goals but didn't follow through. Do you procrastinate, avoid taking risks, or set unrealistically high standards that are impossible to meet? These behaviors can prevent you from achieving your full potential.

Writing in a journal can be an effective way to uncover recurring themes and behaviors. Documenting your thoughts and experiences creates a space for honest self reflection. Over time, patterns that were previously hidden may become clear.

How the Brain Interprets Self-Defeating Behaviors

Your brain has a role in shaping your thoughts and behaviors. It processes information from your environment and forms responses that guide your actions. When you encounter different situations, your brain interprets them based on past experiences and learned patterns. These interpretations influence how you feel and react. Over time, your brain develops habits—some of which may support your growth, while others might hold you back.

The Amygdala and Fear Response

The amygdala is a small, almond-shaped part of your brain that plays a crucial role in processing emotions, particularly fear and anxiety. When you experience something negative or threatening, the amygdala triggers a fear response. This response is designed to protect you by preparing your body to fight, flee, or freeze. However, when faced with situations that aren't genuinely threatening, this fear response can lead to anxiety and stress. For instance, recalling past failures or anticipating criticism can activate the amygdala, causing you to avoid challenges and engage in self-defeating behaviors.

The Prefrontal Cortex and Decision Making

The prefrontal cortex, located at the front of your brain, is responsible for higher-level functions like rational thinking, planning, and decision-making. It helps you weigh the pros and cons of different actions and make informed choices. However, when you are stressed or anxious, the prefrontal cortex's efficiency decreases. Stress hormones can interfere with its functioning, leading to impulsive or poorly thought-out decisions. This can reinforce self-defeating behaviors, as you might choose the easier, less risky path rather than challenging yourself to grow. Strengthening the prefrontal cortex through stress management and mindfulness can improve your decision-making abilities.

Formation of Neural Pathways

Every thought and action you engage in creates neural pathways in your brain. These pathways are like trails in a forest—used paths become clearer and easier to follow over time. When you repeatedly think or act in a certain way, these neural pathways become stronger, making the behavior more automatic. For example, if you habitually procrastinate, your brain becomes wired to delay tasks. This makes it harder to break the habit because the neural pathway is well-established. However, the same principle applies to positive behaviors. Consistently practicing new, healthy habits can strengthen those neural pathways, making positive changes more natural and automatic.

Neuroplasticity and Changing Behaviors

Neuroplasticity is the brain's remarkable ability to reorganize itself by forming new neural connections throughout life. This means you can change your habits and thoughts, regardless of age. When you introduce new, positive behaviors, your brain can create new pathways and weaken old, negative ones. Techniques like mindfulness, which involves staying present and aware of your thoughts, and positive affirmations, which are repeated positive statements about yourself, can aid in this process. These practices help rewire your brain, fostering more constructive and empowering thought patterns and behaviors.

Impact on Brain Chemistry

Your thoughts and behaviors significantly affect your brain chemistry. Negative thoughts and stress can lower neurotransmitters like serotonin and dopamine levels, which are crucial for maintaining a positive mood and overall well-being. Low levels of these chemicals can lead to feelings of sadness, anxiety, and lack of motivation. On the other hand, engaging in positive activities and thinking can boost these neurotransmitters, enhancing your mood and promoting a sense of well-being. Activities such as exercise, social interactions, and practicing gratitude can help improve your brain chemistry.

Practical Techniques for Rewiring the Brain

Mindfulness Practices: Mindfulness involves focusing on the present moment without judgment. It can help reduce stress and increase awareness of one's thoughts and behaviors. Techniques include deep breathing exercises, meditation, and mindful walking. These practices can calm the amygdala and strengthen the prefrontal cortex, helping one manage stress better and make more rational decisions.

Positive Affirmations: Positive affirmations are statements you repeat to yourself to encourage and motivate. For example, saying, "I am capable and strong" can help replace negative thoughts with positive ones. Over time, these affirmations can create new neural pathways, making positive thinking more automatic and reducing self-defeating behaviors.

Cognitive Behavioral Therapy (CBT): CBT is a therapeutic approach that helps you identify and change negative thought patterns. By recognizing irrational or harmful thoughts and challenging them, you can replace them with more balanced and constructive ones. Techniques used in CBT include thought records, where you write down negative thoughts and find evidence against them, and behavioral experiments, where you test out new behaviors to see their effects.

Healthy Habits: Healthy habits like regular exercise, a balanced diet, and sufficient sleep support brain health and positive thinking. Exercise releases endorphins, which are chemicals that improve mood. Eating a nutritious diet provides the necessary nutrients for optimal brain function. Adequate sleep ensures that your brain has the time it needs to process information and recover, which is essential for maintaining mental clarity and emotional balance.

Steps to Change Self-Defeating Behaviors

- **Acknowledge and Name the Behavior:** The first step to change is acknowledging the behavior. Label it when it occurs. This could be as simple as saying, "I am procrastinating," or "I am comparing myself to others again."

- **Understand the Trigger:** Every behavior has a trigger. Identify what sets off your self-defeating behavior. Is it a particular situation, a feeling, or a time of day?

- **Develop New Responses:** Once you know your triggers, you can plan healthier responses. If you typically respond to stress by doubting your abilities, try instead to bolster yourself with affirmations or seek supportive feedback from friends or mentors.

- **Set Small, Achievable Goals:** Break the cycle of self-defeat by setting small goals you can achieve. This builds confidence and reinforces the belief in your capabilities.

What is Self-Love?

Self-love is the acceptance and appreciation of oneself that grows from actions supporting our physical, psychological, and spiritual growth. It means caring for yourself deeply, not just to survive, but to thrive. Self-love enables you to nurture your growth and well-being holistically.

Overcoming self-defeating behaviors is an important step in the journey towards self-love. When you learn to identify and modify these behaviors, you're not just avoiding negative outcomes but actively fostering a positive environment where self-love can flourish. Think about it this way: whenever you challenge a self-critical thought or resist the urge to compare yourself to others, you reinforce your worth and capability. This isn't just beneficial—it's transformative.

For example, if you habitually downplay your achievements because you feel they aren't good enough, recognizing and adjusting this behavior can help you start celebrating your successes, big and small. This shift boosts your self-esteem and solidifies your sense of self-love.

Self-Love vs. Self-Care

While self-love and self-care are deeply interconnected, they are not the same. Self-love is your overall attitude toward yourself—it's the belief in and respect for your own worth. Self-love involves giving yourself compassion and understanding while pushing yourself to grow in the most nurturing way possible.

Self-care, on the other hand, is the set of actions you take to realize the love you have for yourself. It includes any intentional actions you undertake to care for your physical, mental, and emotional health.

How they Complement Each Other

Imagine self-love as the soil and self-care as the water and sunlight needed for a garden to thrive. Without the fertile soil of self-love, self-care practices can feel like chores or temporary fixes. However, with a strong foundation of self-love, self-care practices are more impactful—they reinforce and express the deep respect and affection you have for yourself.

For instance, a self-care practice like attending a weekly yoga class becomes more than just physical exercise; it becomes a reflection of your commitment to maintaining your health and well-being, a critical part of loving yourself.

The Role of Self-Compassion

Developing self-compassion is like learning to be your own best friend, especially in moments of difficulty or self-doubt. This essential component of self-love involves treating yourself with the same kindness, concern, and support you would offer to a good friend. It means accepting that you are human, and like everyone else, you are imperfect. It is also about being gentle with yourself when you confront failures or make mistakes rather than being harshly self-critical. Self-compassion provides emotional resilience, allowing you to acknowledge your flaws and shortcomings with empathy and understanding rather than judgment or self-punishment.

Why is Self-Compassion Important?
Think about how you talk to yourself when you face a setback. Do you immediately criticize yourself or take a moment to comfort yourself? The way you respond can significantly impact your emotional well-being. Self-compassion fosters emotional recovery and provides a buffer against anxiety and depression. It shifts your perspective from a criticism and limitation mindset to encouragement and infinite possibility.

Strategies to Cultivate Self-Compassion

1. Recognize Your Self-Talk: Your internal dialogue plays a crucial role in shaping your self-image. Start noticing the tone of your conversations with yourself. Are they friendly and supportive or critical and demeaning? The goal is to soften this self-talk, making it more compassionate and understanding.

2. Practice Mindfulness: Mindfulness involves being present and fully engaged with the moment, without judgment. When you notice yourself slipping into self-criticism or rumination, use mindfulness to gently acknowledge these thoughts and feelings without identifying with them. This practice helps you gain perspective and respond with compassion.

3. Write Yourself a Letter: When you're struggling, try writing a letter to yourself from the perspective of a compassionate friend. What would this friend say to you? How would they encourage you? This exercise can help shift your perspective and increase your emotional resilience.

4. Use Self-Compassion Breaks: Whenever you find yourself in a moment of stress or self-criticism, take a self-compassion break. Close your eyes, place your hand on your heart, and breathe deeply. Speak kindly to yourself, acknowledging your suffering and reminding yourself of your humanity. These moments can be pivotal in changing your habitual responses.

5. Develop a Compassion Mantra: Create a set of compassionate phrases you can use when you notice yourself being self-critical. Phrases like "I am doing my best," "I am worthy of kindness," or "I accept myself as I am" can be powerful tools to foster self-compassion.

Cultivating an Authentic Self-Identity

Discovering and embracing your true self is one of the most empowering steps you can take. Authentic self-identity is the true expression of who you are beyond societal expectations and personal insecurities. When you act authentically, you align your behaviors with your personal values and desires rather than conforming to external pressures. It's the state of being where you feel most genuinely yourself, without the masks or roles that you might feel pressured to adopt.

Why Authenticity Matters
Living authentically boosts self-esteem, decreases anxiety, improves relationships, and generally increases overall happiness. When you are true to yourself, you create a satisfying and meaningful life.

Steps to Discover Your True Self

1. Reflect on Your Values: What truly matters to you? What principles do you want to live by? Spend some time reflecting on these questions and writing down your core values. This reflection is foundational in building an authentic life.

2. Assess Your Current Life: Look at your current behaviors and life choices. Ask yourself how well they align with your identified values. This might involve examining your career, your relationships, and your hobbies.

3. Listen to Your Inner Voice: We often drown out our preferences to please others or to fit into certain social molds. Start tuning into your own desires by spending quiet time alone, journaling, or meditating.

4. Set Boundaries Based on Your Values: Once you know what's important to you, set boundaries to protect and express these values. If family is a top priority, for example, you might set a boundary around working late hours.

5. Embrace Imperfection: Part of being authentic is accepting that you are not perfect. Allow yourself to make mistakes and learn from them, showing genuine growth and resilience.

Action Items for Personal Growth

- **Daily Values Reflection:** Each day, take a moment to reflect on one value and how you've honored it in your actions. This practice helps to ground your daily activities in your core beliefs and ensures that your actions are continually aligned with what truly matters to you. It's a simple yet powerful way to make your values a living part of every day.

- **Weekly Authenticity Check-ins:** Review your activities and decisions once a week to ensure they align with your true self. Adjust as needed to reflect your values better. This regular audit of your life decisions helps to prevent drift and keeps your actions and goals closely tied to your personal truth and integrity.

- **Create a Vision Board:** Visualize your authentic life by creating a vision board that represents your core values and aspirations. This visual representation can serve as a constant reminder and inspiration, fueling your motivation to act in ways that embody your deepest desires and long-term goals. Place it somewhere you can see daily to keep your vision clear and focused.

Imagine you've always had a passion for art, yet you find yourself in a career that doesn't tap into your creative side—perhaps something practical that was expected of you. Every day, you feel the disconnect between your job and what truly ignites your spirit. What if you decided to make a change? Envision yourself signing up for art classes in the evening. This small step could be transformative, allowing you to explore and express your creativity. As you hold the brush, dip it into paint, and move it across the canvas, each stroke is a reaffirmation of your true self. It's not just an art; it's a rediscovery of what makes you feel alive and fulfilled. This alignment with your authenticity brings immense satisfaction and a profound connection to what you genuinely love.

Reflective Questions

- What are the top five values you want to define your life?
- When do you feel the most like yourself?
- What changes can you make to live more authentically?

As you work through these steps and questions, remember that cultivating an authentic self-identity is a dynamic process. It evolves as you grow and learn more about yourself. Each step you take towards authenticity is a step towards a richer, more fulfilling life.

Implementing Self-Love Daily

Embracing self-love is not just an act you perform; it's a lifestyle you cultivate. Integrating self-love into your daily life means establishing routines and practices that nurture your well-being, counteract self-defeating behaviors, and bolster your self-worth and self-image.

Making Self-Love a Daily Practice
Consistency is key when it comes to self-love. You need to make small, everyday choices to add up to a profound impact on how you see and treat yourself.

A) Start with Self-Awareness

- **Morning Affirmations**: Begin each day by affirming your worth. Stand in front of a mirror, look into your own eyes, and say positive affirmations aloud. Examples include "I am worthy of good things," "I accept myself as I am today," and "I am capable of achieving my goals." This practice sets a positive tone for the day, reinforcing your self-worth right from the start.

- **Mindful Moments:** Incorporate mindfulness into your daily routine. This could be a five-minute meditation in the morning or simply taking deep, mindful breaths during transition moments throughout your day, like before starting your car or after closing your laptop. Mindfulness centers your thoughts and reduces the impact of stress, helping you remain grounded and focused.

B) Cultivate Healthy Relationships

- **Communicate Openly:** Foster open communication in your relationships. Expressing your thoughts and feelings honestly and respectfully shows self-respect and invites mutual understanding. When you communicate your needs and boundaries clearly, you are practicing self-love by ensuring you are heard and respected.

- **Choose Supportive Company:** Surround yourself with people who uplift and support you. Relationships should reinforce your self-esteem, not diminish it. If you find certain interactions consistently drain your energy or self-confidence, it may be time to reconsider these connections.

C) Enhance Your Environment

- **Create a Personal Sanctuary:** Dedicate a space in your home where you can retreat and feel safe, whether it's a cozy corner with books and a blanket or a small garden space. This sanctuary is a physical representation of your commitment to caring for yourself.

- **Declutter Your Space:** Regularly decluttering your living and working spaces can significantly affect your mental clarity and stress levels. A tidy environment reflects and supports a clear, positive mind.

Implement Reflective Practices

- **Journaling:** Keep a daily journal where you track your thoughts, feelings, and achievements. Journaling is an excellent way to reflect on your day, celebrate successes (no matter how small), and process emotions. This habit fosters a deepened self-awareness and appreciation.

- **Review and Reset:** At the end of each day, take a few minutes to review what went well and what could be improved. Setting intentions for the next day can help you stay committed to your self-love goals.

Daily Self-Love in Action

Wake up each morning and start your day with a simple affirmation that speaks to your strengths. Throughout the day, take short breaks to breathe deeply and recenter, ensuring stress does not overwhelm you. When challenges arise, instead of defaulting to self-criticism, treat yourself with kindness, reminding yourself that setbacks are opportunities to learn and grow. In your interactions, speak kindly to yourself and others, reflecting the respect and love you feel for yourself. This daily practice not only enhances your self-esteem but also reinforces a positive, loving approach to life's ups and downs.

Chapter 2: Unraveling the Myths

"The most terrifying thing is to accept oneself completely." – Carl Jung.

Your journey to self-love can often be met with skepticism—not just from the world around us, but from within ourselves. Myths about self-love can cloud our understanding and hinder our progress. In this chapter, we'll confront these myths head-on, debunking misconceptions and shed light on the genuine essence of self-love.

Addressing Common Myths

Myth 1: Self-Love Is Selfish

- **The Reality:** Self-love is not about disregarding the needs of others; rather, it's about ensuring you are well enough to be of service to those around you. Think of it as the safety instructions on an airplane: you must put on your own oxygen mask before helping others. When you care for yourself, you are in a better position to care for those you love.

- **Example:** Picture yourself as a busy mother who constantly puts her own needs last to prioritize her family's. While this might seem noble, over time, you may find yourself feeling exhausted and resentful. However, if you start taking time for self-care and self-love, you'll notice a replenishment in your energy. This allows you to support your family not just dutifully, but joyfully and effectively.

Myth 2: Self-Love Means You Think You're Perfect

- **The Reality:** Self-love is not about believing you are flawless; it's about accepting yourself as you are while recognizing that there is always room for growth and improvement. It's the balance between self-acceptance and self-improvement.

- **Example:** A young professional might struggle with impostor syndrome, feeling undeserving of her position. By practicing self-love, she learns to accept her current skills and also acknowledges her potential to learn and grow, thus overcoming feelings of inadequacy. This acceptance doesn't stop her from striving to improve; instead, it provides a healthy environment where personal development is fueled by kindness and encouragement rather than self-criticism.

Myth 3: Self-Love Can Be Achieved Overnight

- **The Reality:** Self-love is a journey, not a destination. It requires continuous effort and adjustment as you grow and your life changes. Having days where self-love feels more difficult is normal, but perseverance makes it a sustainable part of your life.

- **Example:** A woman may feel empowered to practice self-love after attending a motivational seminar. However, she soon realizes that consistent practice is required. It's not a one-time achievement but an ongoing process of learning and relearning self-love techniques.

Myth 4: Self-Love is All about Pampering

- **The Reality:** While treating yourself to spa days or shopping can be aspects of self-care, self-love is much deeper. It involves nurturing your mind, body, and spirit through practices like setting boundaries, pursuing goals, and engaging in meaningful self-reflection.

- **Example:** A retired teacher finds self-love through volunteering, which reconnects her with her passion for helping others and provides a sense of purpose and fulfillment beyond any physical pampering. This involvement not only enriches her life but also strengthens her sense of community and connection, proving that self-love enhances not just her own well-being but also the lives of those around her. Through giving, she receives the joy and validation from making a meaningful difference.

By debunking these myths, we open the door to a more nuanced understanding of what it means to truly love oneself. In the following sections, we will delve deeper into the truth behind self-love, exploring scientific evidence highlighting its benefits, ensuring that our journey is informed and transformative.

The Truth Behind Self-Love

While the myths surrounding self-love might make it seem elusive or trivial, the reality is far more profound and scientifically supported. Self-love is a practice backed by research that shows its immense benefits for your mental, physical, and emotional health.

The Science and Psychological Benefits of Self-Love

Rooted in psychology and neuroscience, self-love involves nurturing neural pathways that promote positive thinking, resilience, and overall well-being. By engaging in self-love practices, you are enhancing your mood and fundamentally rewiring your brain to embrace a more positive self-image and improved psychological health. Here are some facts you should know:

- **Increased Resilience:** Practicing self-love regularly can significantly boost your resilience. You'll find yourself navigating stress more effectively, bouncing back from failures more quickly, and pursuing your goals with renewed energy. Self-love practices like mindfulness and positive self-talk can rewire the brain, enhancing emotional regulation and stress response. Imagine being a corporate executive who once worked exhaustive 80-hour weeks, believing your self-worth was solely tied to your success. By integrating self-love into your routine, you start to value your well-being just as much as your career. This shift not only reduces your stress but also unexpectedly increases your productivity and job satisfaction.

- **Enhanced Self-Esteem:** Regular self-love rituals helps to boost self-esteem. You naturally develop a stronger sense of self-worth when you consistently treat yourself with kindness and respect. This is not just about feeling better in the moment; it's about building a lasting foundation of confidence. For example, an artist who struggled with self-doubt started practicing morning affirmations and self-compassion exercises. This routine bolstered her confidence and helped her navigate and eventually overcome external criticism, leading to her first successful gallery showing.

- **Reduced Anxiety and Depression:** Engaging in self-love has been linked to lower levels of anxiety and depression. This is because self-love practices help mitigate the internal critic that can drive these feelings. Neuroscientific research supports this by showing that activities like mindfulness meditation can decrease the gray matter in the amygdala, which is involved in the stress response, while increasing gray matter in areas linked to empathy and emotional regulation. (We will have a more detailed discussion on the psychological benefits of self-love in subsequent sections)

Embracing Diversity in Self-Love

The journey to self-love is universal, yet deeply personal, and it doesn't look the same for everyone. Each person's path is shaped by their unique life experiences, cultural background, and personal identity.

Cultural Perspectives on Self-Love

Different cultures can have vastly different views on self-love and self-care. In some cultures, community and family needs may be prioritized over individual desires, which can influence how people perceive and practice self-love. For example, in many Eastern cultures, the concept of self-love is often intertwined with duties to family and community, balancing personal well-being with the well-being of others. Contrast this with more individualistic Western perspectives, where self-love might focus more on individual achievement and personal fulfillment.

Age and Life Stages

The importance of self-love remains constant throughout life, but how we practice it can change as we move through different life stages. The evolution of self-love is crucial to adapt to the changing perspectives and needs that come with each new phase of life:

- **For Young Adults:** Self-love might involve exploring identity, establishing independence, and learning from experiences. At this vibrant stage, you're laying the groundwork for who you will become. It's a time for testing boundaries, making mistakes, and learning invaluable lessons about what truly matters to you. Practicing self-love here means giving yourself grace as you navigate these formative years, encouraging yourself to step out of your comfort zone while also respecting your limits.

- **For Mid-Lifers:** It might focus on self-acceptance, embracing life changes, and nurturing relationships that honor their true self. This period often brings significant life transitions, such as career shifts, parenting changes, or reevaluating life choices. Self-love during these years is about embracing where you are in life, letting go of the unmet expectations from your youth, and appreciating the journey thus far. It's a powerful act of self-love to look at your accomplishments and challenges, acknowledging how they have shaped you.

- **For Older Adults:** Self-love can mean preserving dignity, embracing aging, and reflecting on life with gratitude. As you age, embracing the physical changes and continuing to find joy in daily activities is a profound demonstration of self-love. It's about valuing your life experiences, sharing wisdom with younger generations, and finding contentment in the legacy you are creating. Practicing self-love in later years is also about seeking fulfillment in simpler pleasures and maintaining social and community connections that reinforce a sense of belonging and purpose.

Gender and Sexual Identity

Self-love is vital for everyone, especially for those who might face discrimination or a lack of acceptance due to their gender or sexual identity. It's fundamentally about affirming your worth and your inherent right to happiness, irrespective of societal norms. For someone who feels misunderstood or marginalized because of their identity, embracing self-love is a powerful step toward personal empowerment and resilience.

Just imagine how challenging it can be when the world seems to question your identity. Imagine finding strength in self-love, which allows you to celebrate your uniqueness and affirm your self-worth. This could mean setting aside time each day to engage in activities that make you feel good about yourself or surrounding yourself with people who affirm and support your true self. It's about building a life that feels authentic to you, despite external opinions.

Moreover, self-love encourages you to seek supportive environments and relationships where you can express yourself freely and safely. It enables you to build resilience against negative external influences and helps foster a sense of belonging. This approach doesn't just benefit you—it also sets a precedent for treating others with the same kindness and respect, regardless of their background or identity.

Socioeconomic Factors

Access to self-love resources can vary depending on socioeconomic status. It's important to suggest practices that are accessible to everyone, like simple mindfulness exercises, free online support groups, or community activities. These resources ensure that self-love practices aren't just for those who can afford expensive therapies or wellness retreats, but are available to everyone. Promoting inclusive self-care helps bridge the gap and provides everyone with the tools needed to foster self-compassion and mental well-being, regardless of their economic background.

Practical Tips for an Inclusive Self-Love Practice:

- ***Educate Yourself:*** Learn about different cultural, social, and personal perspectives on self-love. Understanding these varying viewpoints can enhance your empathy and enrich your own practices, allowing you to appreciate the diverse ways people approach self-care and self-acceptance. This education can come from books, documentaries, or engaging directly with communities and individuals.

- ***Be Mindful of Language:*** Use inclusive language that speaks to a diverse audience, recognizing the variety of experiences that influence how we love ourselves. Language shapes perception, so it's crucial to choose words that are respectful and affirming of all identities and experiences. This consideration ensures that everyone feels valued and seen, which is fundamental to promoting genuine self-love.

- ***Customize Your Approach:*** Tailor self-love practices to fit your personal circumstances, considering factors like cultural background, life stage, and personal challenges. Not all practices suit everyone; for instance, meditation might resonate well with some, while others might find journaling more effective. Customizing your approach allows self-love to be more meaningful and effective in your personal context.

- ***Seek Diverse Stories:*** Listen to and learn from the self-love journeys of people from different backgrounds. This can broaden your understanding and deepen your practice of self-love. Hearing about the challenges and successes of others can provide new insights, inspire your own practices, and remind you of the universal need for and benefits of self-love.

Chapter 3: The Psychological Foundations of Self-Love

"To fall in love with yourself is the first secret to happiness." – Robert Morley.

Self-love is a robust psychological tool that enhances our mental health and overall well-being. This chapter will explore the psychological underpinnings of self-love and how it influences our minds, shapes our behaviors, and ultimately, leads us to a more fulfilled life.

Simplifying Complex Research

Psychological research provides compelling evidence that developing a healthy relationship with oneself can significantly improve various aspects of life, from emotional resilience to personal relationships.

Research indicates that individuals who practice self-love tend to have higher levels of psychological well-being. This includes reduced symptoms of anxiety and depression, better stress management, and a greater sense of life satisfaction.

An example of this can be seen in a study where participants who engaged in regular self-affirmation practices experienced marked improvements in their overall mood and reduced stress levels compared to those who did not. These affirmations, simple statements that reinforce personal value and strength, help individuals maintain a positive outlook and cope more effectively with the daily pressures of life, illustrating the tangible benefits of self-love practices on mental health.

Enhancing Self-Efficacy

Self-love nurtures self-efficacy, which is the belief in one's ability to succeed in specific situations. This belief directly impacts motivation, performance, and the willingness to take on new challenges.

- **Practical Tip:** Start each day by listing three things you did well the previous day. This simple exercise can reinforce your confidence and help cultivate a mindset that is prepared to tackle new challenges.

Improving Emotional Intelligence

Self-love encourages a deeper emotional connection with yourself, enhancing your emotional intelligence. This increased awareness can lead to better decision-making and more fulfilling relationships. When you practice self-love, you're more likely to recognize your emotional needs and communicate them effectively to others. This can lead to healthier and more satisfying personal relationships.

The Role of Self-Love in Personal Development

Self-love is a critical component of personal growth and development. Accepting and valuing ourselves sets the foundation for genuine improvement and lasting change.

Fostering Growth Mindset

Self-love shifts the mindset from a fixed perspective, where abilities are seen as unchangeable, to a growth mindset, where challenges are opportunities for growth. This shift is crucial for personal development and achievement.

- **Practical Tip:** Whenever you face a setback, instead of criticizing yourself, ask, "What can I learn from this?" This reframing can transform challenges into valuable learning opportunities.

Encouraging Risk-Taking

Self-love provides the emotional safety net needed to take risks and explore new opportunities without the fear of failure defining your self-worth.

- *Example:* An entrepreneur with a strong sense of self-love is more likely to pursue innovative ideas, knowing that their value does not hinge on the success or failure of a single venture.

Self-love and Mental Health

The connection between self-love and mental health is profound and influential. Embracing self-love enhances your emotional landscape and also fortifies your mental resilience, allowing you to navigate life's challenges with greater ease and confidence. Self-love acts as a protective barrier against common mental health challenges, providing a stronger sense of self and a more stable emotional foundation. This section explores how nurturing love for oneself directly influences mental health.

Reducing Symptoms of Anxiety and Depression

People who practice self-love consistently report lower levels of **anxiety and depression**. This is because self-love encourages a more compassionate internal dialogue, which can significantly alter the way we react to stress and adversity.

- Create a 'self-compassion pause' whenever you feel overwhelmed. This involves taking a moment to breathe deeply, acknowledge your feelings without judgment, and remind yourself of your worth and capabilities.

Strengthening Emotional Resilience

Developing resilience is a crucial aspect of self-love, particularly when considering mental health. Practicing self-love fosters a positive self-view, which is essential for bouncing back from mental setbacks and challenges more quickly. For instance, if you face a situation where you're passed over for a promotion, embracing self-love allows you to treat this setback with kindness rather than self-criticism. By focusing on your accomplishments and maintaining a positive outlook, you nurture your mental health and protect your self-esteem. This self-compassionate approach helps preserve your confidence and resilience, ultimately guiding you to new and possibly better opportunities.

Practical Advice for Enhancing Mental Health Through Self-Love

Cultivating a loving relationship with yourself is a key strategy for sustaining good mental health. Here are some practical ways to integrate self-love into your mental health practices:

Regular Self-Reflection

Regular self-reflection can help you understand your emotional needs and the root causes of distress, fostering deeper self-love and better mental health.

- *Practical Tip:* Keep a reflection journal where you record daily events and how you treated yourself throughout the day. Were you kind and understanding, or critical and demanding? Adjust your self-treatment accordingly.

Set Realistic Expectations

Setting realistic expectations is crucial in practicing self-love. Unrealistic goals can lead to feelings of inadequacy and failure, which are detrimental to mental health. For instance, if you've been holding yourself to the standard of perfection, consider adjusting your expectations to value progress instead. This shift can significantly reduce your stress levels and enhance your enjoyment of both personal and professional life.

Cultivate a Supportive Environment

The environment you create for yourself can significantly influence your mental health. Cultivating a positive, supportive environment reinforces self-love and enhances your mental well-being.

- *Practical Tip:* Regularly evaluate your social interactions. Invest more time in relationships that uplift you and less in those that drain you. Sometimes, self-love means setting boundaries with others to protect your mental health.

Remember, each act of self-love improves your mental well-being and strengthens your capacity to face life's challenges with resilience and grace.

Overcoming Negative Self-Talk

Negative self-talk can be a formidable adversary. They are voices in your head that insist you're not good enough, smart enough, or capable enough and often stems from deeper, sometimes unconscious beliefs developed over years from experiences and external influences. Transforming these thought patterns is crucial, not only for nurturing self-love but for your overall mental and emotional health.

Identify Common Negative Patterns:

- **All-or-Nothing Thinking**: Seeing things in black-and-white categories. If your performance falls short of perfect, you see yourself as a total failure.
- **Overgeneralizing:** Seeing a single negative event as a never-ending pattern of defeat.
- **Catastrophizing:** Anticipating the worst. You spill coffee on your shirt and imagine the entire day going downhill.

Strategies to Counter Negative Self-Talk

Changing how you talk to yourself can profoundly affect your self-esteem and overall mental outlook. Here are some effective strategies to transform negative self-talk into a more positive and supportive internal dialogue:

1. Recognize and Stop:
Become aware of the onset of negative thoughts and actively choose to stop them. This can involve mentally saying "stop" or using a physical gesture like snapping a rubber band lightly on your wrist as a cue to shift your mindset.

- ***Practical Tip:*** Keep a thought diary. Whenever you engage in negative self-talk, write it down, analyze it, and dispute it with evidence that contradicts it.

2. Challenge Negative Thoughts:

Ask yourself:
- "Is this thought really true?"
- "Would I say this to someone I love?"
- "What evidence do I have that supports or contradicts this thought?"

Challenging your negative thoughts helps you see that they are not facts but merely opinions that you can change.

3. Replace Negative Thoughts with Positive Affirmations:
For every negative thought that arises, replace it with a positive affirmation. If you think, "I can't do anything right," counter it with, "I am capable and have succeeded in many tasks."

4. Practice Gratitude:
Focus on the good things in your life. This can shift your mindset from constantly looking for what is wrong to one that notices what is right.

- ***Practical Tip:*** Start or end your day by listing three things you are grateful for. This practice can transform your perspective and reduce the power of negative self-talk.

5. Engage in Positive Activities:
Activities that boost your mood can also help silence negative self-talk. Engage in hobbies, exercise, or social activities that make you feel good about yourself.

So, as you can see! Transforming negative self-talk is about rewriting the narrative of your own life. It's not just about stopping negative thoughts but about creating a new story you tell yourself, where you are the deserving hero, not the perpetual villain.

Remember, the goal isn't to never have negative thoughts but to change how you respond to them. With practice, the voices of self-doubt become quieter, and the voices of self-assurance become your new inner dialogue.

Building Emotional Resilience

Emotional resilience is your ability to bounce back from stress, adversity, failure, challenges, or even trauma. It means facing distress or pain directly, recovering, and growing from the experience. Integrating self-love into your resilience-building practices enriches your capacity to manage life's ups and downs more effectively.

Why is Emotional Resilience Important?

- It reduces the risk of anxiety and depression.
- It improves coping mechanisms in stressful situations.
- It enables you to engage more fully in life, without fear of emotional setbacks.

Cultivating Resilience Through Self-Love

1. Develop a Self-Care Routine:
Consistent self-care is a foundational aspect of building resilience. It can be as simple as ensuring enough sleep, maintaining a nutritious diet, exercising regularly, and setting aside time for relaxation and fun.

- ***Practical Tip:*** Start with small, manageable changes to your routine. Could you wake up *30 minutes* earlier to enjoy a quiet cup of coffee and plan your day? What about introducing a 10-minute meditation or journaling session each night?

2. Set Boundaries to Preserve Energy:
Knowing when and how to say no is crucial. Setting healthy boundaries protects your energy and fosters self-respect.

- ***Example:*** If you often feel overwhelmed by commitments, practice saying no to new requests that don't align with your priorities or current capacities. This isn't selfish; it's a necessary form of self-respect.

3. Practice Mindful Awareness:
Mindfulness teaches you to remain connected to the present moment, helping reduce anxiety about the future or regrets over the past.

- ***Practical Tip:*** Incorporate brief mindfulness exercises into your daily life. For instance, try a five-minute breathing exercise where you focus solely on the sensation of breathing in and out. This can help center your thoughts and reduce feelings of overwhelm.

4. Build Supportive Relationships:
The support of friends, family, or community groups can provide an external source of resilience. Surround yourself with people who uplift and encourage you.

Questions to Consider:

- Who in your life makes you feel good about yourself?
- Are there relationships that drain more than they replenish?

5. Learn From Setbacks:
View failures as lessons, not defeats. Reflect on what didn't work and why, and consider how you can use this knowledge to improve.

- ***Example:*** After a project at work doesn't go as planned, instead of beating yourself up, review the sequence of events and identify areas for improvement and factors for the success to take into your next project.

6. Celebrate Your Wins:
Make it a habit to celebrate your accomplishments, no matter how small. This reinforces positive self-perception and boosts your morale.

- ***Practical Tip:*** Create a 'success journal,' where you note down even the smallest victories. Did you handle a difficult conversation with grace? Write it down and remind yourself of your growth.

Remember, building resilience is a continuous process. Each day presents new challenges and learning opportunities.

Connecting Happiness and Self-Love

The journey to happiness is deeply intertwined with the practice of self-love. Self-love sets the foundation for happiness by fostering an internal environment of acceptance and appreciation. When you love yourself, you are better equipped to experience joy, create meaningful relationships, and engage fully with life. Here are some points where Self-love is Key to Happiness:

- **Inner Harmony:** Self-love quiets internal conflicts and aligns your thoughts with positive emotions, reducing stress and increasing peace of mind.
- **Empowerment:** Loving yourself provides the confidence to pursue what truly makes you happy, rather than conforming to others' expectations.
- **Resilience:** A solid base of self-love helps you rebound from life's setbacks, maintaining your happiness even in challenging times.

Understanding and nurturing the relationship between self-love and happiness will unlock a more joyful, fulfilled existence. Remember, the steps you take to love yourself not only improve your mental and emotional well-being but also your capacity to experience joy each day.

Chapter 4: Childhood and Its Lasting Effects

"The child is the father of the man." – William Wordsworth.

Our childhood experiences lay the foundation for our self-perception and emotional well-being. From our earliest days, the interactions and environments we are exposed to shape how we see ourselves and the world around us.

Early Influences: Shaping Self-Perception

From the moment you are born, your experiences, interactions, and environment begin to shape your views of the world and yourself. Childhood, being a particularly sensitive phase, influences how you perceive yourself in adulthood. Your interactions with family members, caregivers, and peers begin to form the lens through which you see yourself. Positive affirmations, support, and love help build a secure and confident self-image, while criticism and neglect can foster doubts about your self-worth.

How Early Experiences Influence Adult Behavior

The beliefs and self-perceptions we develop in childhood can manifest in our adult behaviors and relationships in several ways:

- **Attachment Styles:** Securely attached children tend to grow into adults who form healthy, independent relationships. In contrast, those with less secure attachments might struggle with dependency or avoidance in relationships.

> Imagine a child growing up in a nurturing and supportive environment where their emotional needs are met consistently. This child learns to trust others and feels safe exploring the world, leading to secure attachment. As an adult, they are likely to form stable, trusting relationships, feeling comfortable with both intimacy and independence.
>
> On the other hand, a child who experiences inconsistent care may develop an anxious attachment style, constantly seeking validation and fearing abandonment in their adult relationships.
>
> Alternatively, a child who experiences neglect may develop an avoidant attachment style, leading them to distance themselves emotionally from others to protect themselves from potential rejection.

- **Self-esteem:** Early experiences that affirm a child's worth foster high self-esteem, whereas negative or dismissive experiences can lead to chronic self-doubt.

  > Think of a child who is frequently praised and encouraged for their efforts and achievements. They are taught to see failures as opportunities to learn rather than as reflections of their worth. This child is likely to grow up with a strong sense of self-esteem, confident in their abilities and resilient in the face of challenges.

Conversely, a child who is often criticized or dismissed may internalize these negative messages, leading to low self-esteem. As adults, they might struggle with chronic self-doubt, constantly questioning their worth and capabilities. They may avoid taking risks or pursuing their goals, fearing failure and rejection.

Emotional Regulation: Children who are taught to understand and manage their emotions in healthy ways often carry these skills into adulthood. Those who are not given the tools to handle their feelings might struggle with emotional regulation later in life.

A child who is encouraged to express their emotions and is guided on how to cope with them – like taking deep breaths when angry, to talk about their feelings instead of acting out, or to find constructive ways to deal with sadness. As adults, they are well equipped to handle stress, communicate their emotions effectively, and maintain emotional balance.

On the other hand, a child who is told to "toughen up" or "stop crying" without any guidance on how to manage their feelings may grow up struggling to deal with emotions. They might resort to unhealthy coping mechanisms, such as substance abuse or aggression, or find it difficult to maintain emotional stability in stressful situations.

- **Relationship Dynamics:** The way we are treated as children often sets the tone for how we expect to be treated in our adult relationships. Positive early interactions can lead to healthier relationship expectations and dynamics.

    Think of a child who is shown consistent love and respect by their parents. They learn to expect kindness, communication, and mutual respect in relationships. As adults, they seek out partners who treat them well and are more likely to have healthy, balanced relationships.

In contrast, a child who witnesses or experiences neglect or abuse may come to see such behaviors as normal or even acceptable. As adults, they might find themselves in unhealthy or abusive relationships, believing they don't deserve better or not recognizing the signs of a healthy partnership.

Reflection Prompts to Uncover Early Influences

- ***Reflect on Key Memories:*** What are your earliest memories of feeling praised or criticized? How do you think these experiences have affected your self-esteem?

- ***Identify Recurring Themes:*** What messages did you receive about your worth, capabilities, and place in the world? How might these messages have shaped your beliefs about yourself?

- ***Consider Your Current Challenges:*** Are there aspects of your self-perception that you struggle with today? Can you trace these back to specific childhood experiences?

Navigating the Impact of Childhood on Self-Love

Recognizing the impact of childhood on your self-perception is the first step towards healing and reshaping your self-image. Here are some strategies to begin addressing these early influences:

Challenge Outdated Beliefs:
As an adult, you have the power to challenge and change the negative beliefs formed in childhood. Question their validity, and replace them with affirmations that reflect your true worth. For instance, if you were often told you weren't good enough, remind yourself daily of your achievements and strengths. Replacing these outdated beliefs with positive affirmations like, "I am capable," "I am worthy of love," and "I am enough" helps you build a more accurate and loving self-view.

Seek Supportive Relationships:
Build relationships with people who recognize and affirm your worth. Positive reinforcement from others can help you rewrite negative perceptions of yourself. Surrounding yourself with encouraging and supportive individuals like friends who genuinely care about you, mentors who guide and inspire you, and support groups that share similar experiences can create a safe space where you feel valued and appreciated.

Engage in Therapeutic Practices:
Consider therapies like cognitive-behavioral therapy (CBT) or narrative therapy to uncover and address deep-seated beliefs about yourself. These therapies can provide tools to reshape your self-perception more healthily. For example, CBT can help you identify and challenge negative thought patterns, while narrative therapy allows you to reframe your life story in a more empowering way.

The Role of Parenting Styles

Parenting styles influence how we develop our self-concept and manage relationships throughout life. Each style carries distinct characteristics and, depending on which one shaped your upbringing, it may have laid the groundwork for how you view yourself and interact with others today.

Parenting styles are typically categorized into four major types, each with its own impact on a child's development:

- **Authoritative:** This style is characterized by warmth, responsiveness, and appropriate discipline. Authoritative parents set clear standards and are communicative with their children, fostering independence along with self-discipline.

- **Authoritarian:** Often confused with authoritative, this style is strict and less responsive. Authoritarian parents enforce rules rigidly and expect obedience without question, often leading to a less supportive environment.

- **Permissive:** These parents are indulgent with few demands. They are extremely loving and thus may encourage self-expression but often lack sufficient boundaries, which can hinder the development of self-discipline.

- **Neglectful:** This style is marked by a lack of responsiveness to a child's needs. Neglectful parents are often emotionally uninvolved and minimally invested in parenting, which can lead to issues with trust and self-esteem in children.

How Parenting Styles Affect You

Reflect on Your Upbringing:
Think about which parenting style best describes your upbringing. How did it influence your feelings of security, self-worth, and your ability to navigate challenges? For instance, children raised by authoritative parents often feel more confident and capable, whereas those raised by authoritarian parents might struggle with self-esteem and decision-making.

- **Example:** If you grew up in a permissive household, you might have appreciated the freedom but also felt a lack of guidance when making important decisions. As an adult, this can translate into difficulties with self-regulation and a tendency to avoid challenges.

Healing and Moving Forward

- **Acknowledge and Accept:** Recognize the strengths and limitations of how you were parented. Accepting these can help you understand your current behavior patterns and emotional responses.

- **Seek Therapy:** Professional help can be invaluable in unpacking the deeper implications of your childhood experiences. Therapies like family systems therapy or psychodynamic therapy can offer insights and tools for healing.

- **Reframe Negative Beliefs:** Identify and actively challenge the negative beliefs you developed about yourself. Replace them with affirmations that affirm your self-worth and capability.

- **Practical Tip:** Write down a list of negative beliefs you hold about yourself. Next to each, write a counter-statement that reflects a more positive and realistic view. For example, change "I must always be perfect" to "It's okay to make mistakes; I learn and grow from them."

- **Cultivate Self-Compassion:** Be kind to yourself. Understand that your behaviors and thoughts are a product of your past experiences and that it's never too late to change and grow.

Questions to Consider:

- How do you envision your life change if you view your childhood experiences as stepping stones rather than stumbling blocks?
- How can you practice self-compassion to counteract the negative impacts of your upbringing?

By exploring and understanding the role of parenting styles in shaping who you are today, you can begin to heal from past wounds and move forward with greater self-awareness and love.

Healing from Childhood Trauma

The shadows cast by childhood trauma can linger long into adulthood, affecting how we see ourselves and interact with the world. Childhood trauma can stem from experiences of neglect, abuse, loss, or witnessing violence. These events can fundamentally alter your sense of safety and self-worth, often manifesting as long-term psychological effects, including anxiety, depression, and relationship difficulties.

Therapeutic Approaches to Healing

Healing from trauma is a deeply personal journey that often requires professional support. Here are some therapeutic approaches that have helped many reclaim their inner peace and self-love.

1. Cognitive-Behavioral Therapy (CBT):

CBT helps address the negative thought patterns that trauma can imprint on your mind. It involves identifying distorted thinking and gradually reshaping these thoughts to support a healthier and more positive outlook on life.

- **Practical Tip:** Start by tracking your thoughts in a journal. When you notice patterns of negative or self-destructive thoughts, challenge them by asking, "Is this thought based on facts or feelings?" and "What would I tell a friend who had this thought?"

2. Eye Movement Desensitization and Reprocessing (EMDR):

EMDR is a powerful therapy designed to alleviate the distress associated with traumatic memories. Through guided eye movements, you can reprocess traumatic memories, significantly reducing their emotional impact. For example, imagine you experienced bullying as a child and those painful memories still cause you emotional turmoil. By undergoing EMDR therapy, you could find that you're able to process these memories without the overwhelming emotions that used to flood in whenever you recalled those difficult times. This therapeutic approach allows you to revisit traumatic events in a safe, controlled environment, ultimately diminishing their power over your present emotional well-being.

3. Narrative Therapy:
Narrative therapy is a transformative approach that involves reframing your understanding of your trauma by telling your story. This method helps you see yourself as separate from your trauma, recognizing your own strength and resilience. For instance, if you've long felt victimized by your past experiences, engaging in narrative therapy could enable you to rewrite your story. Instead of seeing yourself as a victim of your circumstances, you begin to view yourself as a survivor and thriver, empowered by your resilience. This shift not only changes how you perceive your past but also how you approach your future, fostering a sense of agency and self-empowerment that permeates all aspects of your life.

4. Trauma-Informed Yoga and Meditation:
These practices help reconnect with your body, which can often feel like an enemy post-trauma. Yoga and meditation foster mindfulness and bodily awareness, which can help calm anxiety and ground your thoughts in the present.

Steps for Self-Care and Healing

- **Develop a Routine:** Establish a daily routine that includes activities that make you feel safe and cared for. This could be as simple as a morning walk, a nightly bath, or scheduled time for reading or meditation.
- **Build a Support Network:** Surround yourself with people who support and uplift you. Healing is often bolstered in environments where you feel understood and valued.
- **Celebrate Small Victories:** Healing from trauma can be a slow process. Recognize and celebrate small milestones,

like a week of managing anxiety or successfully using a new coping strategy.

Question to Reflect On:

- What small steps can you take today to start healing from past trauma?

Healing from childhood trauma is undoubtedly challenging, but with the right tools and support, it is entirely possible. As you work through these therapeutic approaches and integrate self-care into your daily life, remember that every step forward is a step towards a lighter, more fulfilled self. You are not alone in this journey; each day brings an opportunity to heal, grow, and move closer to the life you deserve.

Re-parenting Yourself: Nurturing Your Inner Child

Re-parenting yourself is about giving your inner child—the deepest, often most vulnerable part of your psyche—the love, care, and attention perhaps you didn't receive sufficiently in your childhood. It involves stepping into the parental role for yourself, providing what was missing in your upbringing, and changing your internal narrative towards a more nurturing and supportive dialogue.

Why Re-parenting?

- **Healing Emotional Wounds:** Nurturing your inner child can help you heal the emotional wounds that linger into adulthood.
- **Correcting Negative Self-Beliefs:** Transform self-criticism into self-compassion by reassessing harmful beliefs about yourself instilled during childhood.

Steps to Begin Re-parenting Yourself

Re-parenting isn't about rewriting your past; it's about affecting your present and future. Here's how you can start this transformative journey:

1. Connect with Your Inner Child:
Identify moments when you feel vulnerable, scared, or upset. These emotions often signal your inner child's presence.

- **Practical Exercise:** Find a quiet space, close your eyes, and picture yourself as a child. What do you see? How do you feel? Speak to your child-self with kindness and reassurance.

2. Validate Your Feelings:
Acknowledging your emotions is crucial in re-parenting. It's about allowing yourself to feel and express your emotions without judgment.

- **Example:** When feeling overwhelmed, instead of ignoring your feelings, you might say, "It's completely okay to feel this way. Let's work through these feelings together."

3. Establish Self-Care Routines:
Just as a caring parent would set routines to ensure a child's well-being, establish routines that prioritize your physical and emotional health.

- **Practical Tip:** Create a morning routine that includes activities nurturing both body and mind, like yoga, journaling, or a nutritious breakfast.

4. Set Healthy Boundaries:

Learning to say no and setting limits is a critical part of re-parenting. It teaches you that your needs matter and helps you protect your energy.

- **Practical Exercise:** Reflect on aspects of your life where boundaries are lacking. Practice setting these by role-playing with a therapist or trusted friend.

5. Foster Joy and Playfulness:
Engage in activities that delight you and ignite your sense of wonder and joy—qualities often vibrant in children.

- **Example:** Schedule regular 'play' times, whether that's a creative hobby, watching your favorite cartoons, or visiting places you loved as a child.

Emotional Reflections for Re-parenting
Ask yourself these reflective questions to deepen your re-parenting process:

- What did I need most as a child that I didn't receive enough of?
- How can I provide that for myself now?
- What words do I wish to hear from a loving parent? How can I start saying them to myself?
- Cultivating Compassion and Understanding

So, as you can see, re-parenting is an act of radical self-love and compassion. It allows you to become the source of your own healing and fulfillment. Remember, this journey isn't about blame; it's about understanding and growth.

The Power of Forgiveness: Embracing Self-Love Through Letting Go

Forgiveness is often misunderstood as a gift to the offender, but in reality, it's a gift to oneself. It's about releasing the burdens of the past to reclaim peace, joy, and freedom in the present. Forgiveness does not mean condoning wrongdoings or forgetting the pain caused. Rather, it's about loosening the grip of resentment and hurt that binds you to the past. It's a deliberate choice to pursue peace, allowing you to move forward unencumbered by anger and bitterness.

Why Forgive?

- **Emotional Relief:** Holding onto anger and resentment can be exhausting. Forgiveness offers emotional liberation, reducing stress and enhancing overall well-being.
- **Improved Relationships:** By choosing forgiveness, you can heal and possibly strengthen relationships, fostering a deeper connection with others and yourself.
- **Increased Happiness:** Letting go of grudges and bitterness opens up space in your heart for more joy and contentment.

Steps to Practicing Forgiveness

Forgiving someone, especially when the hurt runs deep, can be challenging. Here are steps to help you begin this transformative journey:

1. Acknowledge Your Feelings:
Admit to yourself how you truly feel about the situation. Suppressing your emotions can prevent you from moving forward.

- **Practical Exercise:** Write a letter to the person who hurt you. Detail how their actions affected you. You don't need to send it, but putting your feelings down on paper can be a cathartic first step.

2. Decide to Forgive:
Forgiveness is a choice. Make a conscious decision to forgive, not for the offender's sake, but for your peace and happiness.

3. Reflect on the Context:
Sometimes, understanding the circumstances or pressures the other person faces can facilitate forgiveness. This isn't about excusing their behavior but about seeing the full picture.

Questions to Consider:

- What might have influenced their actions?
- Have I ever made a mistake for which I hoped to be forgiven?

4. Actively Let Go:
Releasing the emotional charge from past events is crucial. This might involve rituals, such as burning the letter you wrote or visualizations of letting the pain float away.

5. Embrace Empathy and Compassion:
Try to feel compassion for the person who wronged you. Often, those who hurt others are in pain themselves. Understanding this can ease the process of forgiveness.

6. Reaffirm Self-Love:
Reconnect with yourself. Affirm that past hurts do not define your worth. Engage in self-care practices that reinforce your value and enhance your self-esteem.

Forgiveness as a Path to Healing

As you practice forgiveness, remember that it's a process. Some days, it will feel easier than others, and that's okay. Every step you take towards forgiveness is a step towards freeing yourself from the past and embracing a future filled with peace and self-love.

- **Practical Tip:** Incorporate a daily affirmation related to forgiveness in your routine. Something like, "I choose to forgive and free myself. I deserve peace."

As you can see, forgiveness allows you to survive past hurts and thrive beyond them. Reflect on everything you've learned about childhood influences and healing, carry forward the understanding that forgiveness is not just about the past—it's a continuing gift of freedom and love you give to yourself every day.

Chapter 5: The Relationship Between Self-Love and Body Image

"To be beautiful means to be yourself. You don't need to be accepted by others. You need to accept yourself."– Thich Nhat Hanh.

Societal expectations of ideal beauty standards can distort self-image and challenge self-esteem. This pressure can lead to a cycle of comparison and self-criticism, undermining your sense of self-worth.

Challenging Societal Standards

Societal standards of beauty are not only pervasive but often unrealistic. They promote a narrow and unattainable image that can lead to feelings of inadequacy and self-doubt.

- **The Impact of Media on Body Image:** Every day, we are bombarded with images and messages that suggest happiness and success are linked to a specific appearance. These messages often emphasize thinness, particular body shapes, and sizes, which can lead to a distorted sense of self. Recognizing the powerful influence of media and questioning its validity in the context of real, diverse human bodies is a crucial step in this journey.

- **Diverse Perspectives on Beauty:** Beauty standards can vary dramatically across cultures and communities, which clearly indicates that 'ideal' body types are a social construct rather than an absolute truth. By exposing ourselves to a wider range of beauty standards and embracing diversity in all forms, we can begin to dismantle the narrow definitions that may have shaped our self-perception. This journey is not just about acceptance, but finding joy and liberation in our unique bodies.

Embracing Body Diversity and Inclusivity

One effective way to challenge harmful societal standards is to promote and engage with platforms that showcase a wide range of body types. Support artists, brands, and media that diverge from traditional beauty standards and highlight the beauty in diversity.

Practical Steps to Take:

- **Audit Your Media Consumption:** Critically examine the media you consume. Do you see only one type of body shape or beauty? Try to diversify the sources and types of media you engage with. Follow influencers and creators who celebrate body diversity. This will help you see beauty in all its forms and feel more connected to a broader community.

- **Educate and Discuss:** Talk about body image issues with friends and family. Education and dialogue can be powerful tools for changing perceptions. Encourage open conversations and share resources that promote body positivity. This collective effort can create a supportive environment for everyone involved.

- **Practice Mindful Acceptance:** When you find yourself being critical of your body, pause and practice mindfulness. Remind yourself that your worth is not tied to your appearance. Focus on what your body can do and the experiences it allows you to have. Embrace gratitude for your body's strength and capabilities.

Once you understand and challenge societal standards that influence body image, you can develop a more accepting and loving relationship with your body.

Embracing Body Positivity: Cultivating a Positive Relationship with Your Body

Body positivity is the acceptance of all bodies, regardless of societal ideals of beauty, size, or shape. It advocates for recognizing the value and worth of every body type, challenging the unrealistic standards often portrayed in the media. This mindset allows you to see beauty in diversity and appreciate the uniqueness of every individual. It also helps combat negative self-talk and encourages you to appreciate your body for what it can do rather than criticize its appearance. This shift in perspective can significantly increase your life satisfaction and reduce feelings of inadequacy.

Practical Steps to Foster Body Positivity

- **Celebrate Functional Over Aesthetic:** Focus on what your body can do rather than how it looks. Whether it's the ability to walk, dance, carry groceries, or hug your loved ones, your body is an amazing instrument that deserves appreciation. For example, think about how your legs carry you through a beautiful nature walk or how your arms embrace a loved one after a long day. Celebrating these functional aspects can shift your focus from appearance to the incredible capabilities of your body.

- **Challenge Negative Thoughts:** When you think negatively about your body, pause and reframe those thoughts. If you're criticizing your body for how it looks, try to shift your focus to something it does that you value. For instance, if you find yourself lamenting your body's appearance in a mirror, remind yourself of how your body helps you perform daily tasks, like lifting your children or completing a workout. This practice helps build a habit of positive reinforcement and self-compassion.

- **Dress for Comfort and Joy:** Wear clothes that make you feel good and comfortable. Clothing should make you feel happy and confident, not confined and self-conscious. Experiment with styles and outfits that highlight your favorite features in ways that feel true to you. For example, choose fabrics that feel good on your skin and colors that lift your mood, creating a wardrobe that enhances your sense of well-being.

- **Practice Gratitude for Your Body:** End each day by thanking your body for what it has allowed you to do. Maybe you walked your dog, typed an important email, or prepared a meal. Acknowledging these everyday activities reinforces the value of your physical self beyond aesthetics.

Incorporating these practices into your daily life transforms your body image and deepens your love for yourself. It's a journey towards self-love, encouraging you to celebrate your unique body with all its imperfections and strengths.

Journey to Self-Acceptance: Embracing Your Body

Self-acceptance means acknowledging and valuing yourself as you are without judgment. It involves letting go of the conditions we often place on our self-worth, such as achieving a certain weight, size, or appearance. Self-acceptance liberates you from the negative self-talk and unrealistic expectations that can dominate your thoughts and actions.

Strategies to Cultivate Body Acceptance

Reflect on Your Self-Talk:
Pay attention to how you speak to yourself about your body. Are your thoughts supportive or critical? Begin to consciously replace negative or critical thoughts with affirmations that reinforce your worth and beauty just as you are. For instance, if you catch yourself thinking, "I don't like my thighs," try replacing that thought with, "My legs are strong and allow me to walk and explore the world." Over time, these affirmations can shift your mindset, helping you see your body more positively. You might also try standing in front of a mirror and saying something kind to yourself each day, reinforcing the practice of self-love.

Focus on Your Body's Capabilities:
Rather than fixating on your body's appearance, appreciate what it can do. Whether carrying you through your daily routines or enabling you to engage in activities you love, your body is an incredible instrument deserving respect and gratitude. Think about the joy of playing with your

children, the strength it takes to carry groceries, or the endurance to complete a challenging workout. These capabilities are far more meaningful than mere appearance. Reflect on moments when your body has helped you achieve something significant, like hiking a mountain or recovering from an illness, and honor those experiences as testaments to your body's resilience and strength in activities you love, your body is an incredible instrument deserving respect and gratitude.

Create a Gratitude Journal for Your Body:
Each day, write down three things your body allowed you to do. This could be as simple as providing the strength to get out of bed or the senses to enjoy a delicious meal. Recognizing these daily capabilities can shift your focus from appearance to appreciation. For instance, you might write, "Today, my body allowed me to take a relaxing bath," or "I appreciated how my hands could create a beautiful piece of art." These small but meaningful reflections can help cultivate a deeper appreciation for your body's functionality and the joy it brings into your life.

Engage in Mindful Movement:
Incorporate activities like yoga or gentle stretching into your routine, focusing on the experience of movement rather than exercise for aesthetic goals. Notice how movement feels, celebrate your mobility, and honor your body's needs and limits. For example, during a yoga session, pay attention to how your muscles stretch and your breath flows, appreciating the meditative aspect of the practice. This mindful approach helps you connect more deeply with your body, fostering a sense of gratitude and respect for its capabilities.

Surround Yourself with Positive Influences:
Choose to consume media and engage with people who promote diverse and realistic body images. This exposure can help reinforce your journey towards self-acceptance by affirming that beauty is not one-size-fits-all. Follow social media accounts that showcase body diversity, read books and articles that discuss body positivity, and join communities that support body acceptance.

Overcoming Body Shame: Embracing Self-Compassion and Confidence

Body shame can be a painful emotional experience that affects how you see yourself and interact with the world. To overcome this, it's important to approach your feelings with empathy and understanding.

Techniques to Combat Body Shame

1. Practice Mindful Awareness:
Mindfulness helps you observe your thoughts and feelings without judgment. When you notice shame-filled thoughts, acknowledge them, and gently guide your focus back to positive affirmations about your body. This practice helps reduce the power of negative thoughts over time.

2. Affirmations and Positive Self-Talk:
Create a list of positive affirmations celebrating your body's strengths and beauty. Repeat these affirmations daily to build a positive self-image. For example, "My body is strong and capable," or "I am more than my appearance."

3. Cognitive Restructuring:
This technique involves identifying and challenging harmful thought patterns. When you catch yourself thinking negatively about your body, ask yourself:

- "Is this thought realistic?"
- "Would I say this to someone I love?"
- "What evidence do I have that this thought is true?"

Challenging these thoughts helps you gradually shift to a more positive and realistic view of yourself.

4. Exposure Therapy:
Gradually expose yourself to situations that may trigger body shame but in a controlled and supportive way. For instance, wearing an outfit you love but feel self-conscious about could be a start. Exposure therapy can help decrease the emotional response to triggers over time.

5. Cultivate Body Gratitude:
Focus on what your body allows you to do rather than its appearance. Be grateful for its functionality—walking, breathing, hugging, and laughing. Writing down these gratitudes can deepen your appreciation and counter feelings of shame.

6. Surround Yourself with Positivity:
Engage with media and social groups that promote a positive body image and inclusivity. Limit exposure to unrealistic beauty standards that can trigger shame. Seek out communities, both online and offline, where body diversity is celebrated and accepted. For example, follow social media accounts that highlight body positivity, such as influencers who share their journeys toward self-love and acceptance. Participate in support groups

or workshops that focus on self-esteem and body confidence.

7. Seek Professional Help:
If body shame is overwhelming and affects your quality of life, consider seeking help from a therapist who specializes in body image issues. Therapy can provide you with tools to deal with deep-seated emotions and guide you toward a healthier self-image.

8. Share Your Feelings:
Talking about your feelings with trusted friends or family members can be liberating. Often, you'll find that you are not alone in your struggles, and sharing can be a powerful step towards healing.

Overcoming body shame is a journey towards self-acceptance. Each step you take builds resilience and fosters a more compassionate relationship with your body. Remember, your body is your ally, not your enemy, and learning to love it in all its forms is a profound act of self-love that can transform your overall happiness and well-being.

Celebrating Your Body: Learning to Appreciate Your Physical Self

Celebrating your body is an essential component of self-love. It's about embracing every curve, edge, and unique detail with gratitude and joy. Here are practical strategies to help you cultivate a mindset that honors and appreciates your body:

1. Dress to Celebrate
Wear clothes that make you feel confident and happy. Choosing outfits that fit well and highlight your favorite features can significantly boost your mood and self-esteem. See dressing as a way to celebrate your body, not conceal it.

2. Engage in Joyful Movement
Find a form of physical activity that you genuinely enjoy, not just for the sake of exercise but for the pleasure it brings. Whether dancing, yoga, walking, or playing a sport, moving your body should feel like a celebration, not a punishment.

3. Practice Gratitude for Body Functionality
Shift your focus from how your body looks to what it can do. Be grateful for the way it carries you through life's tasks. For example, you might say, "I'm thankful for my hands that allow me to write, cook, and hug my loved ones."

4. Create a Body Appreciation Journal
Keep a journal dedicated to noting what you appreciate about your body daily. This can help shift your focus from criticism to admiration and remind you of your body's many positive aspects during tougher days.

5. Mindful Eating
Adopt a mindfulness attitude when you eat. This involves appreciating the flavors, textures, and smells of your food and recognizing the nourishment it provides. Mindful eating helps strengthen a positive connection with food and your body.

Celebrating your body is an ongoing practice, not a one-time event. It requires consistency and commitment but becomes more natural over time. As you continue implementing these strategies, you'll likely notice how you feel about your body – a shift towards more joy, appreciation, and profound acceptance.

Chapter 6: Self-Love in Relationships

"Love yourself first and everything else falls into line. You really have to love yourself to get anything done in this world." – Lucille Ball.

The Foundation of Mutual Respect

When you value yourself, you naturally instill a level of respect that others are likely to mirror. Consider how a strong sense of self-worth makes you less likely to tolerate disrespect or neglect. It's not about ego; it's about knowing what you deserve and expecting to be treated accordingly.

Enhancing Relationship Satisfaction

Practicing self-love also enhances overall relationship satisfaction because it prevents dependency by filling your own emotional needs. This allows you to enter relationships not out of necessity but out of desire for mutual growth and enjoyment. Mutual growth refers to the process of both partners supporting and encouraging each other's personal development, while mutual enjoyment involves sharing experiences and creating happy memories together. For instance, when you feel fulfilled independently, your relationships are no longer about filling a void but sharing happiness with someone else.

The Ripple Effect of Self-Love

The influence of self-love extends beyond personal benefits—it also positively affects those around you. People will often notice your respect for yourself and may be inspired to treat themselves and others better. This creates a cycle of positivity, improving the quality of your relationships and encouraging a more considerate and respectful environment.

Cultivating Positive Interactions:

- **Communicate Openly and Honestly:** Start by expressing your needs and feelings clearly in your relationships. This honest communication fosters deeper connections and mutual respect.
- **Choose Compassionate Feedback:** When addressing issues, approach them from a place of understanding rather than blame. This helps maintain a supportive environment even during disagreements.

Setting Healthy Boundaries: Essential Strategies for Personal Well-Being

Boundaries are the guidelines you set to define how others are allowed to treat you. They reflect your values, priorities, and self-respect, helping you manage what you accept in your relationships and what you don't. Establishing strong boundaries is essential for your mental and emotional health because it protects you from being exploited or manipulated by others. Here are seven benefits:

- **Promotes Self-Respect:** Setting boundaries demonstrates that you value yourself and your needs. It sends a clear message to others that you won't tolerate disrespect or mistreatment, reinforcing your sense of self-worth.

- **Enhances Emotional Well-Being:** Boundaries help you manage stress and emotional overload by preventing others from imposing their demands and expectations on you. This control over your interactions supports a healthier emotional state.

- **Prevents Burnout:** By clearly defining your limits, you avoid overcommitting and taking on too many responsibilities. This balance is crucial for maintaining your energy levels and overall well-being.

- **Fosters Healthy Relationships:** Boundaries ensure relationships are based on mutual respect and understanding. They help you build connections where your needs and feelings are acknowledged and valued, leading to more fulfilling and balanced relationships.

- **Protects Against Manipulation:** Strong boundaries make it harder for others to exploit or manipulate you. By knowing and enforcing your limits, you reduce the risk of being taken advantage of in personal or professional situations.

- **Promotes Personal Growth:** Establishing and maintaining boundaries requires self-awareness and assertiveness. This practice encourages personal development as you learn to effectively advocate for yourself and your needs.

- **Increases Self-Confidence:** Successfully setting and upholding boundaries boosts confidence. This empowerment comes from knowing you have the right to control your life and interactions, fostering a stronger sense of autonomy.

How to Identify Your Personal Boundaries

Start by reflecting on past experiences where you felt discomfort, resentment, or exhaustion. These emotions often signal that your boundaries were crossed. Ask yourself:

What exactly made me feel uncomfortable?
Pinpoint specific actions or behaviors that triggered your discomfort. Was it someone's tone of voice, the nature of their request, or the setting of the interaction? Identifying these details helps clarify what you need to avoid or change in the future.

Why did that interaction leave me feeling drained?
Analyze the underlying reasons for your emotional exhaustion. Were you giving too much of your time or energy without receiving support in return? Did you feel pressured to meet someone else's expectations at the expense of your own needs?

What would I need to prevent this in the future?
Think about practical measures you can take to protect yourself. This might involve setting limits on how much time you spend with certain individuals, clearly communicating your needs, or deciding not to engage in activities that drain you.

These questions can help you pinpoint where you need to set clearer limits.

Steps to Establishing Boundaries

1. **Clearly Define Your Limits:** Be specific about what you can tolerate and accept in your relationships. These limits include your physical space, emotional energy, time, and personal values. For instance, if you find it draining to communicate late at night, set a boundary to not accept calls after a certain hour. Additionally, if you need time alone to recharge, let others know you need some quiet time each day. Understanding these personal limits helps you stay true to yourself.

2. **Communicate Your Boundaries Clearly:** Once you know what your boundaries are, the next step is to communicate them clearly to others without ambiguity. Use assertive communication, which involves expressing your needs and feelings in a direct and respectful manner. This is different from aggressive communication, which involves forcing your needs onto others, or passive communication, which involves not expressing your needs at all. For example, you could say, "I value our conversations, but I need to stop taking calls after 9 PM so I can wind down and get some rest." This communicates your boundary clearly and respectfully, without leaving room for misinterpretation.

3. **Anticipate Potential Pushback:** Be prepared for the possibility that others may not immediately accept your boundaries. Understand that some people might need time to adjust, and that's okay. For example, if a friend insists on discussing sensitive topics you're uncomfortable with, you might say, "I understand you want to talk about this, but I'm not ready to discuss it now. Let's revisit it later."

4. **Reevaluate and Adjust as Needed:** Boundaries are not static and can change over time as your needs and circumstances evolve. Periodically review your boundaries to ensure they still serve you well. For example, if you initially set a boundary to avoid weekend work but find an occasional Saturday morning meeting necessary, adjust your boundary to accommodate that change while still protecting your personal time.

Tips for Maintaining Boundaries

- **Be Consistent:** Consistency is key when maintaining boundaries. If you're inconsistent, others may push your boundaries to test your limits. Regularly reinforcing your boundaries helps others understand your needs and shows that you respect yourself. For example, if you've set a boundary to not work past 6 PM, make it a point to log off at that time every day, regardless of external pressures.

- **Handle Boundary Violations Firmly:** If someone repeatedly disrespects your boundaries, address the issue directly and firmly. Explain how their behavior affects you and reiterate your boundaries. If necessary, be prepared to take further action, such as distancing yourself from the situation or relationship. For instance, if a colleague continually interrupts your work with non-urgent requests, you might say, "I need to focus on my work during office hours. Please save non-urgent matters for our scheduled meetings."

- **Practice Self-Care:** Maintaining boundaries can be emotionally taxing. Ensure you are practicing self-care, which reinforces the importance of your boundaries and helps you stay resilient in the face of challenges. For example, schedule regular breaks throughout your day, engage in activities that relax and rejuvenate you, and seek support from friends or a therapist if needed. This helps you recharge and reinforces your commitment to your boundaries.

- **Seek Support When Needed:** Don't hesitate to ask for help from trusted friends, family, or professionals when you struggle to maintain your boundaries. They can provide encouragement, advice, and even intervene if someone persistently violates your boundaries. For instance, a close friend might support you during difficult conversations, reinforcing your boundaries to others.

- **Celebrate Your Progress:** Acknowledge and celebrate your progress in setting and maintaining your boundaries. Recognizing your efforts and achievements boosts your confidence and reinforces your commitment to maintaining healthy boundaries. For example, treat yourself to something special when you successfully uphold a challenging boundary, reinforcing the positive impact of your efforts on your well-being.

Keep in mind that setting boundaries clarifies what you need to thrive and what others can expect from you. This clarity enhances harmony in your relationships, allowing you to connect with others genuinely and wholeheartedly.

Exiting Toxic Relationships: Embracing Freedom and Self-Respect

My journey began in the shadows of an oppressive and abusive marriage, a place where I felt more like a prisoner than a partner. Navigating through toxic relationships demands both courage and a deep commitment to self-love.

What is a toxic relationship?
A toxic relationship is characterized by behaviors that are emotionally and, sometimes, physically damaging to one partner. It often involves patterns of manipulation, control, and disrespect. You may feel constantly undermined, experience frequent conflicts, or find that your emotional needs are consistently unmet and dismissed.

Signs to Watch For:

- Consistent feelings of unhappiness and dissatisfaction in the relationship.
- Feeling drained instead of energized by your interactions.
- Fear of expressing your true feelings and opinions.
- Recurring disrespect for your boundaries.

Steps to Safely Exit Toxic Relationships

Acknowledge the Toxicity:
The first step to breaking free from a toxic relationship is acknowledging that it is harmful. This can be incredibly challenging, especially if there are moments of happiness or if manipulation confuses your perceptions. For example, you might start keeping a journal to document instances of toxic behavior, helping you see patterns and recognize the negative impact on your well-being. This clarity is essential for taking the next steps toward a healthier life.

Seek Support:
Confiding in trusted friends, family, or a professional can give you the support and perspective needed to make difficult decisions. They can offer emotional support and help you see the situation more clearly. For instance, joining a support group for people in similar situations can provide a sense of community and validation, making you feel less alone and more empowered to take action.

Plan Your Exit and Identify Safe Places:
Leaving a toxic relationship can be complex, especially if it involves cohabitation or financial entanglement. Planning your exit strategy is crucial. This might include setting up a separate bank account, finding somewhere else to live, or consulting a counselor or legal advisor. Additionally, plan where you will go after leaving the relationship. This might be the home of a friend or family member, a shelter, or another safe space. Knowing exactly where you can go reduces uncertainty and increases your safety when moving. Create a checklist of tasks and a timeline to ensure a smooth transition, such as arranging temporary housing with a trusted friend while you search for a permanent solution.

Establish and Maintain Boundaries:
Once you decide to leave, clearly communicating your boundaries is essential. If safe, let the other person know that the relationship is no longer healthy for you and that you must end it to take care of your well-being. For example, you might say, "I need space to focus on my mental health, and I won't be responding to your messages for a while." Setting these boundaries helps you maintain your decision and protect your mental health.

Focus on Self-Care:
Exiting a toxic relationship is emotionally taxing. Engage in activities that reinforce your self-worth and invest time in healing. Whether reconnecting with hobbies you love, practicing mindfulness, or simply allowing yourself time to

rest, it's vital to nurture your well-being during this time. Consider seeking therapy or counseling to process your emotions and develop coping strategies for the transition period.

Secure Personal Documents and Finances:
Ensure all your important documents and financial assets are secure. This includes personal identification, bank documents, credit cards, and any legal papers. If possible, set aside emergency funds that only you can access. This step is crucial in maintaining your independence and security. For example, store these documents in a safe place, such as a safety deposit box or with a trusted friend, to ensure they are accessible when needed.

Utilize Legal Resources:
If the situation involves abuse, harassment, or threats, it may be necessary to seek legal protection. Contact local authorities or legal professionals to discuss options such as restraining orders. Understanding your legal rights can provide additional security as you navigate your exit. For example, you might work with a lawyer to draft a restraining order and ensure that law enforcement is aware of your situation to provide prompt assistance if needed.

Create a Support Network: In addition to your close friends and family, reach out to support groups and community resources that can offer guidance and assistance. Organizations dedicated to relationship abuse or counseling can provide emotional support and practical advice to help you through this time. For instance, local shelters or nonprofits often offer counseling services, legal advice, and safe housing options for individuals escaping toxic relationships.

Permit Yourself to Leave Gradually: Sometimes, immediate departure isn't possible or safe. If this is the case, develop a gradual plan of leaving. This might involve slowly moving your belongings, securing housing and employment in a new city, or spending less time at home incrementally. Whatever the strategy, ensure it prioritizes your safety and well-being. For example, start by staying with friends on weekends and progressively extend your time away until you can fully transition out of the relationship.

Reconnect with Your Support System:
Rebuilding your life after leaving a toxic relationship involves reconnecting with your support system and rediscovering your interests and passions. Engage with friends and family who uplift you and participate in activities that bring you joy and fulfillment. This can include hobbies you neglected, joining clubs or groups that interest you, or taking classes to learn something new. This reconnection helps reestablish your identity and reinforces your self-worth, providing a solid foundation for moving forward.

Each of these steps is designed to support and protect you as you take decisive action to leave a toxic relationship. Remember, prioritizing your safety and well-being is not selfish—it's necessary. These actions can be challenging but essential to reclaiming your independence and finding peace. Once free from the toxic relationship, focus on rebuilding stronger, healthier connections.

Prioritizing Self-Love: Foundation for Healthy Relationships

You have seen the significance of embracing self-love not just a personal victory but essential for building and maintaining healthy, fulfilling relationships. Now, let's explore some practical ways to prioritize self-love to enhance your relationships.

Daily Self-Affirmations
Begin each day by affirming your worth. Use affirmations like "I am worthy of respect and love," or "I am enough just

as I am." These positive statements can boost your self-esteem and set a positive tone for your interactions with others. Over time, these affirmations can rewire your thinking patterns to be more positive and self-affirming. Incorporating this practice into your morning routine can help you start each day with confidence and clarity.

Set Aside Time for Self-Reflection
Regularly spend time alone reflecting on your goals, boundaries, and feelings. This practice helps you maintain a strong sense of self and ensures your relationships align with your personal values. For example, journaling your thoughts can provide insights into your emotions and decision-making processes. This self-awareness fosters healthier interactions by making you more attuned to your needs and desires.

Cultivate Self-Compassion
Be kind to yourself, especially during tough times. Treat yourself with the same compassion you would offer a friend. This kindness strengthens your emotional resilience, helping you interact with others from a place of strength and stability. When you make mistakes, remind yourself that imperfection is part of being human. Self-compassion can reduce stress and improve overall well-being, positively impacting your relationships.

Engage in Activities You Love
Make time for hobbies and activities that bring you joy and fulfillment. Doing things you love boosts your mood and self-esteem, which can enhance your interactions with others. Whether painting, hiking, or reading, these activities provide a sense of accomplishment and relaxation. Sharing your passions with others can also create deeper connections and mutual understanding.

Prioritize Your Health
Take care of your physical and mental health through regular exercise, a nutritious diet, and adequate sleep. A healthy body and mind are crucial for maintaining the

energy and positivity needed for healthy relationships. Engaging in regular physical activity can reduce stress and improve your mood. Prioritizing your health also sets a good example for those around you, encouraging them to take care of themselves as well.

Seek Constructive Feedback
Ask for feedback from trusted friends or family about improving your relationship skills. This shows a commitment to personal growth and self-improvement. Listening to others' perspectives can provide valuable insights and help you identify areas for development. Make sure to approach feedback with an open mind and a willingness to change, which can strengthen your relationships.

Celebrate Your Accomplishments
Take time to acknowledge and celebrate your achievements, no matter how small. Recognizing your successes reinforces your self-worth and reminds you and others of your value. Celebrating milestones can boost your confidence and motivate you to pursue further goals. Share your achievements with loved ones to foster community and support.

Practice Mindfulness
Stay present in your interactions with others. Mindfulness helps you respond more thoughtfully and less reactively, which can lead to more meaningful and respectful relationships. Practicing mindfulness can involve techniques like deep breathing or meditation. We'll discuss mindfulness in more detail in the subsequent sections.

Building Supportive Connections

Your relationships should provide comfort, joy, and mutual understanding, creating a foundation where both parties can thrive. Here are ten practical strategies to help you nurture relationships that enrich your life and the lives of those around you.

- **Communicate Openly and Honestly:** Ensure your communication is clear and open. Share your thoughts and feelings honestly but respectfully, encouraging a two-way dialogue where both parties feel heard. For example, if something bothers you, address it calmly and openly, rather than letting resentment build up. This approach fosters trust and mutual respect in the relationship.

- **Show Genuine Interest:** Take an active interest in the lives of others. Ask questions about their experiences, thoughts, and feelings. This strengthens connections and shows that you value them as individuals. For instance, remember details about their hobbies or recent activities and follow up on these in future conversations. This attentiveness demonstrates your genuine care and appreciation for their uniqueness.

- **Be a Good Listener:** Listening is crucial to building supportive relationships. Listen to understand, not to respond, which shows that you value what they have to say and are engaged in the conversation. Practice active listening by nodding, maintaining eye contact, and providing feedback. Reflect back on what you've heard to ensure understanding, such as saying, "It sounds like you're feeling..."

- **Offer Help Selflessly:** Be there to offer help when your friends or family need it, without expecting anything in return. Acts of kindness can significantly strengthen bonds. Whether helping with a move, offering a listening ear, or assisting with a project, these gestures show that you are reliable and supportive, fostering a deeper sense of trust and connection.

- **Celebrate Their Successes:** Be enthusiastic about the successes of others. Celebrate their achievements with genuine joy and pride, which can foster a supportive and uplifting relationship. For example, send a congratulatory message or organize a small celebration to acknowledge their milestones. Your encouragement helps them feel valued and appreciated, reinforcing positive feelings within the relationship.

- **Encourage Their Goals and Dreams:** Support others in pursuing their goals and dreams. Offer encouragement and, where possible, practical help or advice, showing that you believe in their potential. This might involve providing resources, brainstorming ideas, or simply offering words of affirmation. Your support can boost their confidence and motivation, demonstrating your investment in their happiness and success.

- **Maintain Consistency:** Be consistent in your interactions and the attention you give. Regular check-ins and consistent behavior build trust and show you are reliable and truly invested in the relationship. Consistency might mean scheduling regular meet-ups or calls, and being present and engaged during these times. This reliability helps establish a stable and dependable foundation for your relationship.

- **Respect Their Boundaries:** Understand and respect the boundaries others set. This respects their needs and helps create a safe and trusting environment for the relationship to flourish. For instance, if someone needs space, honor their request without pushing for immediate interaction. Recognizing and valuing their limits shows respect and consideration, which strengthens mutual trust and comfort in the relationship.

- **Share Experiences:** Create shared experiences, whether they're simple outings, vacations, or just regular catch-ups. Shared experiences can create lasting memories and deeper bonds. Plan activities that you both enjoy, such as hiking, cooking together, or attending events. These moments of connection foster a sense of togetherness and build a reservoir of positive shared memories.

- **Address Conflicts Constructively:** When conflicts arise, handle them with patience and a focus on finding solutions. Address issues directly with those involved and seek to resolve them in a way that strengthens the relationship rather than diminishing it. Use "I" statements to express your feelings without blaming the other person, and strive to understand their perspective as well. This approach encourages open dialogue and mutual problem-solving, which can reinforce the strength and resilience of your relationship.

Reflective Questions for Self-Improvement
As you work on building supportive connections, consider these questions to guide your efforts:

- How often do I contact others to check how they are doing?
- Do I listen as much as I speak when I'm with someone?
- What can I do to show genuine interest and appreciation for the people in my life today?

Incorporating these strategies can be as simple as sending a thoughtful message to a friend or scheduling regular meet-ups. For example, you could make it a point to ask more in-depth questions during your conversations to better understand the perspectives and challenges of those around you. Each small step contributes to a richer, more supportive network of relationships.

Chapter 7: Self-Love and Career Success

"To achieve greatness, start where you are, use what you have, do what you can." – Arthur Ashe.

Success in your career is significantly influenced by how much you value yourself. Your self-worth can empower you to seek out and thrive in professional environments that respect and enhance your inner value.

Aligning Work with Self-Worth

Finding a career that mirrors your self-esteem involves seeking roles that resonate with your values, utilize your skills, and contribute to your personal growth. Here's how you can start aligning your career with your self-worth:

- **Identify Your Values:** Define what values are most important to you in a professional setting. Is it creativity, stability, leadership, service, innovation? Understanding your core values can guide you in finding careers that align with what truly matters to you. For instance, if you value service, you might seek roles in non-profits or healthcare. Identifying these values ensures your work is fulfilling and aligns with your principles.

- **Assess Your Skills and Talents:** Evaluate your skills and talents honestly. Recognizing your strengths can boost your confidence and help you identify job opportunities where your abilities will be valued and nurtured. Create a list of your key skills and past achievements to see where you excel. This can guide you towards roles that fit your talents and provide opportunities to further develop them.

- **Seek Environments That Support Growth:** Look for workplaces offering personal and professional growth support. This could be through training programs, mentorship, or policies encouraging work-life balance. Environments that prioritize employee development are more likely to appreciate and foster your worth. For example, a company that provides regular training sessions and career advancement opportunities is committed to nurturing its employees' growth.

- **Reflect on Your Past Experiences:** Consider your previous job experiences—what aspects did you enjoy, and what felt diminishing? Reflecting on these can clarify what environments and roles are likely fulfilling and which ones to avoid. For instance, if you thrive in collaborative projects but felt restricted in highly hierarchical structures, seek workplaces that value teamwork and flexible leadership styles.

- **Network with Like-Minded Professionals:** Networking with individuals who share your values and have similar career aspirations can provide insights and open doors to opportunities that align with your self-worth. Attend industry meetups, join professional groups, or participate in forums related to your career interests. For example, joining a professional association in your field can connect you with mentors and peers who support your career goals and values.

- **Articulate Your Worth in Job Applications and Interviews:** When applying for jobs, tailor your CV and cover letter to highlight how your values and skills align with the company's culture and the role's requirements.

During interviews, confidently express how your background and expertise make you a valuable asset to the team. For instance, if you value innovation, discuss specific projects where your creative solutions made a significant impact. This alignment shows potential employers that you are qualified and a great fit for their team.

- **Regularly Reevaluate Your Career Path:** Your personal and professional growth should lead to periodic reassessing of your career path. As you evolve, your understanding of your self-worth will also change, which might lead you to seek new challenges or shifts in your career. For instance, if you initially sought stability but now crave new challenges, you might consider transitioning to a more dynamic role or even a new industry. Regularly reflecting on your career ensures it aligns with your evolving self-worth and aspirations.

- **Cultivating a Career That Respects Your Worth:** By actively seeking and creating opportunities that align with your self-worth, you enhance your career satisfaction and reinforce your self-esteem. Each step taken towards aligning your work with your values and capabilities is a step towards a more fulfilling and successful professional life. Remember, you deserve to work in an environment that sees and appreciates your true worth.

Combating Impostor Syndrome

Impostor syndrome can feel like an invisible barrier to success, with persistent doubts about your abilities and the fear of being exposed as a fraud gnawing at your confidence. It is the belief that you're not as competent as others perceive you to be. It's common among high achievers who find it difficult to accept their accomplishments.

Strategies to Overcome Feelings of Inadequacy

- **Acknowledge Your Feelings:** Start by acknowledging that these feelings exist. Understanding that impostor syndrome is a known experience can help you realize you're not alone in this struggle. Accepting these thoughts is part of a common phenomenon that can reduce their power over you. Recognizing and naming these feelings is important to begin addressing them effectively.

- **Reassess Your Competencies:** List all your qualifications, accomplishments, and experiences. Reviewing this list can help you see the hard evidence of your abilities and remind you of your right to be in your position. For instance, list out your degrees, certifications, completed projects, and positive feedback you've received. This tangible record serves as a counterbalance to feelings of inadequacy, reinforcing your competence.

- **Share Your Feelings:** Talk about your feelings with trusted colleagues, mentors, or friends. You'll likely find that many have felt the same way at some point, and they can offer reassurance and perspective.

Sharing your experiences can open up supportive conversations and reduce the isolation that impostor syndrome often brings. It also helps to hear how others have navigated similar feelings.

- **Reframe Failure as a Learning Opportunity:** Instead of viewing mistakes as evidence of inadequacy, see them as opportunities to learn and grow. This shift in perspective can reduce the pressure to perform perfectly. For example, if you make an error at work, analyze what went wrong and what you can do differently next time. This approach turns setbacks into valuable experiences that contribute to your growth.

- **Set Realistic Expectations:** Be realistic about what you can achieve and recognize that everyone has limitations. Setting attainable goals can help you feel more confident about meeting them. Break larger tasks into smaller, manageable steps, and set deadlines that reflect a realistic pace. This can prevent you from feeling overwhelmed and help you see your progress more clearly.

- **Celebrate Small Wins:** Take time to celebrate your achievements, no matter how small. This can help build your confidence over time and reinforce the recognition of your own success. For instance, after completing a challenging project, treat yourself to something enjoyable or simply take a moment to acknowledge your hard work. Celebrating these moments reinforces a positive view of your capabilities.

- **Practice Self-Compassion:** Be kind to yourself. Remember that perfection is impossible, and everyone has moments of doubt. Treat yourself with the same compassion you would offer a friend in your situation.

For example, if you're feeling down about a mistake, remind yourself that it's okay to be imperfect and focus on what you can learn from the experience. Self-compassion helps build resilience and a healthier self-image.

- **Visualize Success:** Spend time visualizing yourself succeeding in your tasks. This mental rehearsal can boost your confidence and help mitigate feelings of fraudulence. Imagine completing a presentation smoothly or receiving praise for your work. Visualization can make success feel more attainable and real, reducing anxiety and self-doubt.

- **Seek Professional Help if Needed:** If impostor syndrome significantly impacts your life, consider seeking help from a psychologist or therapist who can provide professional strategies to combat these feelings. A mental health professional can offer techniques such as cognitive-behavioral therapy (CBT) to help you reframe negative thoughts and build confidence. They can also help you develop personalized coping strategies.

- **Keep a Success Journal:** Maintain a journal where you regularly document your successes and positive feedback. Reviewing this journal can provide a tangible reminder of your skills and achievements. Include details of your accomplishments, colleague compliments, and moments of personal pride. This practice helps create a positive narrative about your professional journey and counters feelings of inadequacy with evidence of your competence.

Questions for Self-Reflection

- What achievements am I most proud of?
- When have I felt like an impostor, and what triggered those feelings?
- How can I change my reaction to mistakes and setbacks?
- Integrating Confidence into Your Career

By actively combating impostor syndrome, you can build a more accurate self-assessment and a robust foundation of confidence. Over time, you'll feel more secure in your role and empower yourself to take on new challenges with a strong belief in your capabilities.

The Power of "Saying No": Empowerment through Selective Commitment

Learning to say no goes beyond simply declining offers or invitations; it's an exercise in self-empowerment and gaining control over your time and resources. Saying no can be challenging, especially when you worry about disappointing others or fear missing out on opportunities. However, being selective about your commitments is crucial for maintaining your mental health and ensuring you don't overextend yourself. It allows you to stay true to your priorities and gives you the space to focus on what truly matters to you.

Strategies for Empowering Yourself through Saying No

- **Evaluate Your Priorities:** Before you can effectively start saying no, you need to clearly understand your priorities. Assess your personal and professional goals and decide how much time and energy you are willing to devote to different activities. For instance, if your primary focus is on advancing your career, you might prioritize work-related commitments over social engagements. This clarity helps you make informed decisions about where to allocate your resources.

- **Practice Assertiveness:** Being assertive means expressing your feelings and needs directly and honestly, without aggression. Practice phrases like, "I appreciate your offer, but I can't commit to this as I have other priorities at the moment." This straightforward approach is respectful yet firm. Over time, assertiveness can help you communicate more effectively and establish clearer boundaries with others.

- **Offer Alternatives:** When saying no, you might feel more comfortable offering an alternative. For instance, if a colleague asks for help with a project, you could say, "I can't help with this right now, but I can review your work next week if you still need input." Offering alternatives shows that you are still willing to support them in a way that fits your schedule, maintaining positive relationships while respecting your own limits.

- **Understand the Value of Your Time:** Recognize that your time is valuable and treat it as such. Reflect on whether a commitment is worth your time and energy and what you might have to give up in your personal life to meet this commitment. For example, consider whether attending a meeting will benefit your career or personal growth or take time away from important family activities or self-care.

- **Set Clear Boundaries:** Communicate your boundaries to others. Let them know what types of requests or invitations you are not currently accepting and explain why. This clarity can prevent future misunderstandings. For example, you might tell your colleagues, "I'm focusing on a major project right now, so I'm limiting new commitments until it's completed."

- **Learn to Be Comfortable with Discomfort:** Saying no can feel uncomfortable at first, especially if you're used to saying yes to please others. Acknowledge this discomfort, but don't let it deter you. Over time, this feeling will lessen as you become more accustomed to prioritizing your needs. Accept that feeling uneasy is okay, and remind yourself that prioritizing your well-being is worth it.

- **Rehearse Your Responses:** If you anticipate a situation in which you'll need to say no, rehearse what you'll say beforehand. Being prepared can make you feel more confident in your response when the time comes. Practice in front of a mirror or with a friend so your delivery feels natural and assured when you need to decline a request.

- **Reflect on Past Experiences:** Think about times when you said yes but wished you had said no. How did that make you feel? Reflecting on these experiences can strengthen your resolve to say no in the future. For instance, if agreeing to a project led to burnout or stress, use that memory to remind yourself why it's important to prioritize your well-being.

- **Reward Yourself:** When you successfully say no, and it leads to a positive outcome, such as more free time or reduced stress, reward yourself. This reinforcement can motivate you to continue practicing this skill. Treat yourself to something enjoyable, like a favorite activity or a small gift, to celebrate your commitment to self-care.

- **Seek Support:** If you find it difficult to say no, seek support from friends, family, or a mentor. Discussing your challenges can provide encouragement and practical advice on handling similar situations. A support system can offer new perspectives and strengthen your confidence in making decisions that align with your priorities.

Finding Work-Life Balance: Harmonizing Professional Goals and Personal Well-being

Achieving work-life balance is crucial for maintaining health, happiness, and productivity. It involves managing your professional and personal life so that neither is neglected. Start by looking honestly at how you currently allocate your time between work and personal activities. Are you spending late nights at the office? Do weekends disappear into work projects? Recognizing your current patterns is the first step towards creating a more balanced life.

Strategies for Achieving Balance

Set Clear Boundaries:
Define specific work hours and stick to them. Inform colleagues and clients about your availability, and be sure to log off and step away from your workspace at the end of your workday. This helps create a clear separation between work and personal time, allowing you to recharge. For instance, if you decide that work ends at 6 p.m., make it a rule not to check work emails or take calls after that time. Setting these boundaries ensures that your personal time is protected and respected.

Prioritize Tasks:
Use prioritization techniques such as the Eisenhower Box to distinguish between urgent and important tasks, important but not urgent, urgent but not important, and neither. This helps you focus on what truly needs your attention each day. By prioritizing effectively, you can tackle high-impact tasks first and avoid the stress of last-minute deadlines. For example, completing a

crucial project report early in the week can prevent a frantic rush as the deadline approaches, giving you more control over your schedule.

Delegate:
Don't hesitate to delegate tasks when possible. This can free up your time and allow you to focus on work that only you can do or that you find most fulfilling. Delegating tasks to team members helps you manage your workload, empowers others, and promotes teamwork. For example, assigning routine data entry tasks to an assistant allows you to focus on strategic planning or creative projects that require your unique skills.

Schedule Downtime:
Just as you schedule meetings and deadlines, schedule regular intervals for relaxation and leisure activities that help you recharge, such as reading, practicing yoga, or spending time with loved ones. Block out time in your calendar for these activities and treat them as non-negotiable appointments with yourself. For instance, if you enjoy morning runs, schedule them into your week to ensure you have dedicated time for physical exercise and mental relaxation.

Make Use of Flexible Work Arrangements:
If your job allows, utilize flexible working arrangements such as telecommuting or adjusted hours to better accommodate your personal life. Flexible schedules can help you manage both professional responsibilities and personal commitments more effectively. For example, starting your workday earlier might allow you to finish in time to attend your child's school events or evening classes.

Streamline Work Processes:
Look for ways to increase efficiency at work through better organization or technology. Reducing time spent on repetitive tasks can lead to more free time to enjoy life. Implementing tools like project management software, automated workflows, or even simple to-do lists can help streamline your tasks. For instance, using an app to automate routine email responses can save you significant time each week.

Cultivate Healthy Work Relationships:
A supportive workplace can significantly enhance your work-life balance. Build relationships with colleagues, leading to a more enjoyable and cooperative work environment. Positive interactions with coworkers can reduce stress and increase job satisfaction. For example, having a reliable team you can count on during busy periods can make work more manageable and less overwhelming.

Communicate Openly with Your Employer:
Have an open conversation with your employer about your work-life balance needs. Many employers will accommodate reasonable requests to keep a team member happy and productive. Discuss options such as flexible hours, remote work, or adjusted workloads. For instance, if you're feeling overwhelmed, a conversation about temporarily reducing your workload or shifting some responsibilities can make a big difference in your balance.

Regularly Review Your Work-Life Balance:
Regularly assess how balanced you feel. What's working well? What's feeling off-kilter? Adjusting your strategies over time can help you maintain balance as your personal and professional needs evolve. Set aside time each month to reflect on your

balance and make necessary adjustments. For example, if you notice that work has started encroaching on family time, you might need to reassess your boundaries or delegate more tasks.

Practice Self-Care:
Ensure that self-care is a non-negotiable part of your routine. It's not just about physical health; mental and emotional well-being are just as important. Incorporate activities that promote relaxation and joy, such as hobbies, exercise, or mindfulness practices. For instance, daily meditation can help reduce stress and improve your overall well-being, making it easier to manage work and personal life demands.

Questions for Self-Evaluation

- How do I feel at the end of the workday?
- What activities do I wish I had more time for?
- Am I regularly feeling drained or energized?

Once you implement these strategies, you can create a fulfilling balance between your professional ambitions and personal happiness, leading to a more satisfying and productive life.

Recognizing Your Achievements: Celebrating Your Successes

Acknowledging your successes is essential for building self-confidence and motivating yourself to continue striving towards your goals. Let's explore how you can effectively recognize and celebrate your achievements, which can reinforce your sense of accomplishment and drive.

The Importance of Celebrating Success

- ***Solidifies Connection between Effort and Outcome:*** Recognizing your achievements helps reinforce the link between the hard work you put in and the positive results you achieve.

- ***Boosts Morale:*** Celebrating successes can significantly enhance your mood and motivation, keeping you energized and focused on your tasks.

- ***Enhances Self-Esteem:*** Acknowledging your accomplishments improves your confidence and self-worth, making you more resilient to challenges.

- ***Inspires Colleagues and Peers:*** Celebrating your successes can motivate and encourage those around you to strive for their own goals.

- ***Reminds You of Progress:*** Celebrating milestones makes your achievements real and tangible, reminding you of your progress towards your larger goals.

Strategies to Acknowledge Your Accomplishments

1. Keep a Success Journal:
Maintain a journal where you regularly write down your achievements, no matter how small. This can range from completing a project on time, making a new business connection, or simply managing a challenging day at work.

2. Set Milestones:
Break larger goals into smaller milestones and celebrate each time you reach one. This can involve anything from a small treat to a day off. Celebrating these smaller victories keeps your motivation high and your focus sharp.

3. Share Your Successes:
Don't hesitate to share your accomplishments with others. Whether with family, friends, or colleagues, sharing can multiply your sense of achievement and encourage others to pursue their goals.

4. Reflect on Your Journey:
Regularly look back at where you started and how far you've come. This reflection can provide a profound sense of accomplishment and motivate you to keep pushing forward.

5. Reward Yourself:
Associate significant achievements with meaningful rewards. Whether it's a weekend getaway, a new book, or a special meal, choose something that feels celebratory and acknowledges the effort you've put in.

6. Use Positive Affirmations:
Reinforce your achievements with positive affirmations. Phrases like "I am capable and successful" can boost your self-esteem and help cement belief in your abilities.

7. Visualize Your Achievements:
Spend time visualizing your completed goals. This mental imagery can reinforce the reality of your achievements and enhance your internal celebration.

8. Educate Others:
Use your experience to mentor others. Sharing your knowledge not only cements your own achievements but also helps others on their paths to success.

9. Update Your Professional Profiles:
Keep your professional profiles and resumes updated with your latest achievements. This will not only help you in career advancement but also serve as a public acknowledgment of your capabilities.

10. Conduct Regular Reviews:
Set aside time for regular reviews of your achievements. This can be monthly, quarterly, or annually, and can help you see the bigger picture of your progress.

Remember, every success, big or small, is a step forward in your journey and deserves acknowledgment and recognition.

Chapter 8: Practical Steps to Cultivate Self-Love

"Loving yourself isn't vanity. It is sanity." – Katrina Mayer.

Daily Actionable Self-Love Practices

1. Morning Routine
Begin each morning by listing three things you are grateful for about yourself. This could be qualities, achievements, or simply acknowledging your effort to face another day. Gratitude shifts your focus from what you feel you lack to the abundance already in your life. Create personal affirmations that resonate with your desires and aspirations for self-acceptance and love. Repeat these affirmations daily to reinforce positive self-talk and reduce negative thoughts.

Steps to Execute This Practice:

Gratitude Journal:
- Keep a journal by your bedside.
- Each morning, write down three things you are grateful for about yourself.
- Reflect on these items and feel the gratitude.

Create Personal Affirmations:
- Write down affirmations that resonate with your goals.
- Place them where you will see them frequently, like on your mirror or phone screen.

- Repeat these affirmations several times throughout the day, especially when feeling negative.

Mindful Breathing:
- Set aside five minutes in the morning and a few times throughout the day.
- Sit comfortably, close your eyes, and focus on your breathing.
- Inhale deeply through your nose, hold for a few seconds, and exhale slowly through your mouth.

Reflect and Adjust:
- At the end of each week, review your gratitude entries and affirmations.
- Adjust your affirmations and add new gratitude points as needed.

2. Personalize Your Space

Surround yourself with items that uplift you. This could be photos, inspirational quotes, or any object that makes you feel happy and at peace. A personalized space can serve as a daily reminder to engage in self-love.

Steps to Execute This Practice:

Identify Items:
- Choose photos of loved ones, places that make you happy, or achievements you're proud of.
- Select inspirational quotes that resonate with you.

Decorate Your Space:
- Arrange these items on your desk, walls, or any visible area in your home or workspace.
- Add joyous objects, such as plants, artwork, or souvenirs.

Organize for Peace:
- Keep your space clutter-free to enhance the sense of calm and order.
- Regularly clean and organize to maintain a serene environment.

Create a Self-Love Corner:
- Dedicate a specific area for self-reflection, meditation, or reading.
- Equip it with comfortable seating, soft lighting, and calming scents like candles or diffusers.

Regular Updates:
- Periodically refresh the space with new photos, quotes, or items to keep it inspiring.
- Rotate objects to reflect your current mood and goals.

3. Connect with Nature

Spend a few minutes outside each day, whether walking in the park, gardening, or simply sitting under a tree. Nature has a calming effect and can help you feel grounded and connected to the world.

Steps to Execute This Practice:

Daily Walks:

- Schedule a daily walk, even if it's just for 10-15 minutes.
- Choose a natural setting like a park or a tree-lined street.

Gardening:
- Start a small garden or tend to indoor plants.
- Spend time each day caring for your plants, which can be meditative.

Outdoor Meditation:
- Find a quiet spot outside to sit and meditate.
- Focus on the sounds of nature and your breathing.

Lunchtime Outdoors:
- Have your lunch outside when possible.
- Use this time to unwind and enjoy the natural surroundings.

Weekend Nature Activities:
- Plan weekend activities like hiking, visiting botanical gardens, or going to the beach.
- Immerse yourself in nature to recharge for the week ahead.

4. Nourish Your Body

Choose at least one meal a day during which you focus on nourishing your body with foods that make you feel good. Pay attention to the flavors and textures, and appreciate the nourishment they provide.

Steps to Execute This Practice:

Plan Your Meals:
- Plan nutritious meals in advance.
- Include a variety of fruits, vegetables, lean proteins, and whole grains.

Mindful Eating:
- Choose a meal to eat without distractions.
- Focus on the flavors, textures, and aromas of your food.

Hydrate:
- Drink plenty of water throughout the day.
- Add natural flavors like lemon or cucumber to make hydration enjoyable.

Cook at Home:
- Prepare meals at home to ensure they are nutritious and made with love.
- Experiment with new recipes that excite you.

Listen to Your Body:
- Pay attention to how different foods make you feel.
- Adjust your diet to include more of what makes you feel energized and healthy.

5. Move Your Body

Engage in physical activity that you enjoy. It doesn't have to be intense or time-consuming. Even a short walk, dance session, or stretching can improve your mood and show your body love.

Steps to Execute This Practice:

Find Enjoyable Activities:
- Identify physical activities you enjoy, such as dancing, swimming, or yoga.
- Incorporate a mix of activities to keep things interesting.

Set a Routine:
- Schedule regular exercise sessions, aiming for at least 30 minutes a day.
- Stick to a consistent routine that fits your lifestyle.

Incorporate Movement into Daily Life:
- Take short breaks to stretch or walk during work.
- Use stairs instead of elevators and walk or bike for short errands.

Join Classes or Groups:

- Participate in exercise classes or sports groups for motivation and social interaction.
- Online classes can also be a convenient option.

Celebrate Progress:
- Track your physical activity and celebrate milestones.
- Acknowledge the positive impact of movement on your mood and health.

6. Digital Detox

Set aside time each day to unplug from digital devices. This can help reduce anxiety and provide you with space to engage more fully with yourself and your immediate environment.

Steps to Execute This Practice:

Designate Device-Free Times:
- Choose specific times of day to unplug, such as during meals or an hour before bed.
- Stick to these times to establish a routine.

Create Tech-Free Zones:
- Establish areas where digital devices are not allowed in your home, like the bedroom or dining area.
- Use these spaces to relax and connect with loved ones.

Engage in Offline Activities:
- Replace screen time with activities like reading, journaling, or outdoor hobbies.
- Explore new interests that don't involve technology.

Use Apps Wisely:
- Utilize apps that track and limit your screen time.

- Set goals for reduced usage and monitor your progress.

Reflect on Benefits:
- Notice how unplugging affects your mood and stress levels.
- Adjust your digital habits based on these observations to enhance your well-being.

7. Self-Care Rituals

Create a regular self-care ritual, such as a warm bath, reading a book, or practicing a skincare routine. This acts as a physical manifestation of self-love and provides a regular reminder to care for yourself.

Steps to Execute This Practice:

Choose Your Ritual:
- Select activities that make you feel relaxed and rejuvenated.
- Examples include taking a bath, reading, meditating, or skincare routines.

Schedule Regularly:
- Set aside specific times for your self-care rituals.
- Treat these times as important appointments with yourself.

Create a Comfortable Environment:
- Set up a space that feels soothing and comfortable.
- Use calming scents, soft lighting, and relaxing music to enhance the experience.

Stay Consistent:
- Make self-care a regular routine, not just an occasional treat.
- Consistency reinforces the importance of taking care of yourself.

Reflect on Benefits:
- Notice how regular self-care rituals impact your mood and overall well-being.
- Adjust your practices to best suit your needs and maximize their benefits.

As you can see, integrating these practices into your daily routine allows you to thrive, not just survive. Remember, self-love is the key to a happier, healthier, and more fulfilled life. Each act of self-love is a declaration of your worth and a step towards lasting happiness.

Mindfulness and Self-Love: Cultivating Presence and Compassion

Mindfulness involves becoming acutely aware of the present moment, enhancing self-love by promoting a nonjudgmental acceptance of your thoughts and feelings. It's rooted in meditation but has become a broader practice that can be applied to various aspects of daily life.

Types of Mindfulness Practices

- *Focused Attention Meditation:* This involves focusing on a single point. This could be your breathing, a specific word or phrase (mantra), a fixed gaze on an object, or the sensations in a part of your body. The goal is to refocus on the chosen point of attention each time you notice your mind wandering.

- *Open Monitoring Meditation:* Unlike focused attention, which narrows your consciousness to one element, open monitoring meditation involves observing all aspects of your experience, moment to moment. Here, you take note of your thoughts, feelings, and sensations without attachment or judgment.

- *Mindful Awareness in Daily Activities:* You can practice mindfulness throughout your day by fully engaging with and paying attention to your routine activities, such as eating, showering, or walking. The key is to be completely present and absorb all aspects of the task at hand.

Creating a Self-Love Ritual Using Mindfulness

- *Choose Your Focus:* Decide what mindfulness practice resonates most with you. It might be a focused attention meditation in the morning or integrating mindful awareness into activities like your daily commute or meal times.

- *Create a Dedicated Space:* Set up a space in your home to engage in your mindfulness practice undisturbed. This could be a small corner with a comfortable seat, some candles, or even a selection of calming music.

- *Schedule Time:* Dedicate a specific time of day for your practice. Early morning or evening can be ideal as these times are generally quieter and conducive to reflection.

- *Start Small:* Begin with short periods, even just five minutes a day, and gradually increase the time as you become more comfortable with the practice.

- *Reflect and Journal:* After each session, reflect on your experience and journal any insights or feelings that arose. This can enhance your self-awareness and deepen your self-love journey.

Affirmations for Confidence: Enhancing Self-Esteem Through Positive Statements

Affirmations are powerful tools in your self-love arsenal. When repeated frequently, they are positive statements that can reinforce self-belief and boost confidence. They work by gradually rewiring your thought patterns, shifting from negative or self-limiting beliefs to a more empowered and positive mindset.

How to Craft Effective Affirmations

1. Keep It Positive:
Focus on what you want to achieve or feel, not what you want to avoid. Use positive language to reinforce what you are affirming. For example, instead of saying, "I am not afraid of speaking in public," use "I am confident and clear when speaking in public."

2. Be Present:
Phrase your affirmations in the present tense as if they are already true. This helps you accept the affirmations as real, influencing your subconscious to act on them. Say, "I am successful and respected in my career," rather than "I will be successful and respected."

3. Make It Personal:
Tailor your affirmations to your specific needs and aspirations. The more personal your affirmation, the more impactful it will be. Consider what aspects of confidence you struggle with and address them directly.

4. Keep It Realistic:
While affirmations should be positive and aspirational, they must also be believable. If an affirmation feels too far-fetched, it can have the opposite effect, reinforcing doubts instead of dispelling them.

Examples of Affirmations to Boost Confidence:

- "I am worthy of love and respect from myself and others."
- "I trust my intuition and make wise decisions."
- "I am capable of achieving my goals."
- "Every day, I grow stronger and more confident."

5. Morning Ritual:
Start your day by repeating your affirmations aloud. Stand in front of a mirror, look yourself in the eyes, and speak your truths. This can set a positive tone for the day ahead.

6. Affirmation Reminders:
Place post-it notes with your affirmations in visible spots around your home and workspace—like on your bathroom mirror, computer monitor, or fridge. These will serve as constant reminders throughout the day.

7. Meditation Incorporation:
Incorporate affirmations into your meditation or mindfulness practice. As you settle into a calm state, repeat your affirmations mentally. This can deepen their impact as you're in a receptive state of mind.

Journaling for Self-Discovery: Unlocking Inner Wisdom

Journaling is a powerful tool for self-reflection and personal growth, enabling you to explore your thoughts, feelings, and experiences in a structured way. It involves writing down your thoughts, feelings, and experiences regularly. It is a private space where you can freely express yourself, explore your emotions, and reflect on your life. This practice can take many forms, each suited to different needs and goals.

Types of Journaling

- **Expressive journaling:** Focuses on expressing thoughts and emotions and is often used for processing life events and emotional healing.

- **Gratitude Journaling:** Writing down things you are grateful for each day can shift your focus from negativity to positivity.

- **Bullet Journaling:** Combines elements of planning, tracking, and reflecting in a highly organized way, helping you keep track of your goals and tasks.

- **Art Journaling** *combines* drawings, collages, and other visual art expressions with written words, ideal for visual thinkers.

- *Dream Journaling:* Involves recording dreams upon waking to explore the subconscious mind's symbols and messages.

The Importance of Journaling

- *Enhances Self-Awareness:* Journaling helps you track patterns and changes over time, providing insights into your behavior and reactions.

- *Facilitates Emotional Release:* Acts as a safe outlet for emotions, reducing stress and anxiety by allowing you to express and understand your feelings.

- *Boosts Memory and Comprehension:* Writing things down improves your ability to absorb and retain information.

- *Encourages Creativity and Problem-Solving:* Freewriting and brainstorming in a journal can spark new ideas and foster creative solutions to challenges.

- *Strengthens Self-Discipline:* Regular journaling cultivates discipline and routine, which can benefit other areas of life.

Integrating Journaling into Your Self-Love Practice

Make journaling a daily ritual. Choose a quiet time and place where you can write without interruptions. Whether first thing in the morning or right before bed, find a time that suits your schedule and stick to it.

Journal Prompts to Get Started:

- What are three things I am grateful for today?
- What is one challenge I faced today, and how did I handle it?
- What are the qualities I like most about myself?

- Describe a moment today when I felt proud of myself.
- What is something I learned today?

Techniques for Effective Journaling:

- *Be Honest:* Write freely and truthfully. Remember, this is your private space.
- *Be Detailed:* Include details to vividly describe your thoughts and experiences.
- *Reflect:* After writing, spend a few minutes reflecting on what you've written. What insights can you gather?

Keep your journaling fresh and engaging by varying your methods. Try different types of journaling or incorporate multimedia elements like photos or sketches. Review your entries periodically to reflect on your growth and understanding. This ongoing dialogue with yourself deepens your self-love and enhances your life's clarity and purpose.

Chapter 9: Overcoming Obstacles to Self-Love

"Obstacles do not block the path, they are the path." – Zen Proverb.

Every journey towards self-love is bound to encounter obstacles. Recognizing and overcoming these barriers is not just a challenge; it's an integral part of the path to deeper self-understanding and acceptance.

Identifying Blockers: Techniques for Recognizing and Addressing Self-Love Obstacles

Understanding what impedes your path to self-love is the first step toward overcoming these challenges. Here are some techniques to help you identify and tackle these obstacles, ensuring they don't hinder your progress toward a fulfilling relationship with yourself.

Unpack Past Failures

Past failures can significantly impact your self-esteem and willingness to take new risks. They can create a mental block where fear of repeating the past inhibits growth.

Technique:

- **Reframing Failure:** Use journaling to write about past failures from a different perspective. Focus on what you learned from each situation rather than what went wrong.

Example: If you once failed to secure a job after an interview, write about what the experience taught you about interview techniques or how it clarified your career goals.

Challenge Limiting Beliefs

Limiting beliefs are those that constrain us in some way. Just by believing them, we do not think, do, or say the things that they inhibit, and in doing so, we impoverish our lives.

Technique

- **Belief Questioning:** Identify a limiting belief and actively question its validity. Ask yourself, "Is this belief based on facts or assumptions? Is there evidence that contradicts this belief?"

- **Example:** If you believe "I'm not talented enough to advance in my career," list the achievements and skills you have acquired over time that prove otherwise.

Address Fear of Rejection

Fear of rejection can prevent you from taking necessary personal development risks or entering into potentially rewarding relationships.

Technique

- **Exposure Therapy:** Gradually expose yourself to small risks that involve potential rejection. Over time, this can help desensitize your fear.
- **Example:** Start by expressing minor disagreements in meetings or social settings, which carries a low risk but helps build your tolerance for opposition or rejection.

Confront Comfort Zones

Staying within your comfort zone can feel safe but often prevents personal growth and self-love by limiting experiences and confidence-building opportunities.

Technique

- Comfort Zone Expansion: Regularly commit to doing something that stretches your comfort zone slightly.
- Example: If public speaking terrifies you, start speaking more during small group gatherings or workshops before progressing to larger audiences.

Each obstacle you conquer brings you closer to a deeper, more fulfilling relationship with yourself. Use these techniques to guide your self-love journey, transforming obstacles into stepping stones.

Handling Setbacks: Sustaining Self-Love Through Challenges

Life's journey often involves setbacks that can test your resolve and shake your self-worth. Maintaining self-love during these times involves deeply understanding and supporting yourself through the ups and downs. Setbacks can come in many forms—whether a career hurdle, a personal loss, or a failed relationship. These moments can feel like steps backward. However, with the right mindset and tools, you can navigate these challenges without losing sight of your self-love.

Strategies for Maintaining Self-Love Through Challenges

1. Accept Your Emotions:
Allow yourself to feel whatever emotions arise without judgment. Acknowledge that it's okay to feel disappointed, sad, or frustrated. Accepting your feelings is the first step in processing them healthily.

2. Practice Self-Compassion:
Be kind to yourself. Remind yourself that setbacks are a normal part of life and do not reflect your worth. Speak to yourself like you would to a friend in a similar situation.

3. Reframe the Experience:
Try to view setbacks as opportunities for growth. Ask yourself what you can learn from this experience and how it can make you stronger or wiser.

4. Maintain Your Routines:
During turmoil, keep up with your regular self-care routines as much as possible. Whether it's your morning jog, meditation session, or a weekly call with a friend, these routines can provide comfort and stability.

5. Set Small, Manageable Goals:
When you're ready, set small goals to help you regain control and progress. Achieving these can boost your confidence and remind you of your capabilities.

6. Seek Support:

Don't hesitate to seek support from friends, family, or professionals. Sharing your struggles can lighten your emotional load and provide you with different perspectives and solutions.

Questions for Self-Reflection

- What can this setback teach me about myself or my approach?
- How can I show myself compassion right now?
- What's one small step I can take today to move forward?
- Integrating These Strategies into Your Life

Start by integrating one or two of these strategies into your life. For instance, begin by practicing acceptance of your emotions for a week. Once you feel comfortable with that, incorporate self-compassion into your daily self-talk. Over time, these strategies will build on each other, strengthening your resilience and deepening your self-love, regardless of your external challenges.

Dealing with Loneliness: Embracing Solitude and Cultivating Self-Compassion

Loneliness can be challenging, often accompanied by feelings of isolation and disconnection. However, experiencing loneliness also provides an opportunity to explore solitude as a space for personal growth and self-compassion.

Understanding Loneliness

Loneliness is a state of mind that causes people to feel empty, alone, and unwanted. It can result from various situations, such as:

- **Physical Isolation:** Moving to a new city, living alone, or working remotely can physically separate us from others.
- **Emotional Isolation:** Feeling misunderstood or different, experiencing a breakup, or losing a loved one.
- **Social Changes:** Changes in social circles, such as friends relocating or changing lifestyles, can also lead to feelings of loneliness.

Finding Strength in Solitude

Solitude, unlike loneliness, is the state of being alone without being lonely. It can be a powerful experience filled with opportunities for self-discovery and inner peace.

> **Reframe Your Perspective:** Start by reframing solitude as an opportunity rather than a deficit. Recognize this time as a chance to engage with yourself deeply and learn more about your desires, thoughts, and feelings.

Create a Comforting Routine: Develop a routine that you find comforting and enriching. This could include reading, gardening, painting, or cooking. These activities can be therapeutic and help you enjoy your own company.

Practice Mindfulness: Engage in mindfulness exercises to ground yourself in the present moment. Mindfulness can help reduce feelings of loneliness by connecting you with the universal human experience of existing moment by moment.

Decorate Your Personal Space: Make your living space a sanctuary that reflects your personality and comforts your soul. A pleasant environment can make solitude feel more like a choice and less like a condition.

Speak Kindly to Yourself: Be mindful of how you talk to yourself during loneliness. Use kind, compassionate self-talk to soothe feelings of isolation. For example, remind yourself, "It's okay to feel lonely. I'm not alone in feeling this way."

Connect Virtually: Use technology to your advantage by connecting with friends and family via video calls, social media, or even old-fashioned letters. Sometimes, a simple conversation can alleviate feelings of isolation.

Volunteer: Volunteering can be a wonderful way to connect with others and reduce feelings of loneliness. It also provides a sense of purpose and community.

Attend Community Events: Look for events in your community that resonate with your interests. Attending workshops, classes, or local gatherings can help you meet new people with similar interests.

Consider Professional Help: If loneliness feels overwhelming, consider seeking help from a mental health professional. Therapy can provide tools and strategies to cope with loneliness and develop more fulfilling social interactions.

Questions for Self-Discovery

- What activities make me feel most connected to myself?
- When do I feel the loneliest, and what can I learn from these moments?
- How can I reach out to others in a way that feels authentic and fulfilling?

Each step you take to understand and alleviate your loneliness enhances your relationship with yourself and prepares you for richer connections with others. Remember, being alone does not have to mean being lonely.

Balancing Expectations: Staying True to Yourself Amid External Pressures

Expectations can come from various sources, including family, friends, the workplace, society, and even within ourselves. They can range from how we should behave and what milestones we should achieve to broader expectations like career success and personal life choices.

Strategies for Managing Expectations

1. Identify and Differentiate Expectations: Start by listing the expectations placed upon you and those you place on yourself. Identify which ones align with your values and goals, which ones feel imposed and misaligned with your authentic self.

For Instance, your parents might expect you to pursue a career in law, but you're passionate about the arts. Recognizing this discrepancy is the first step in addressing and reconciling these expectations.

2. Communicate Your Boundaries: Once you identify which expectations do not align with your values, communicate your boundaries to those involved. Be clear about what is and isn't acceptable to you.

3. Prioritize Self-Reflection: Spend time regularly reflecting on your desires and goals. This self-reflection will help you understand what truly matters to you, independent of external influences.

4. Learn to Say No:
Saying no is a powerful tool for managing expectations. It allows you to set clear limits around what you are willing and unwilling to do based on your priorities and values.

5. Seek Support:
Find allies, whether friends, colleagues, or support groups, who understand and support your need to live authentically. A support system can give you the strength to deal with others' pushback.

6. Adjust Your Self-Expectations:
Be gentle with yourself and recognize when your own expectations are unrealistic. Adjust them to be more in line with your current abilities and circumstances.

7. Celebrate Your Choices:
Whenever you make a decision that honors your true self, take a moment to celebrate it. This reinforces the value of staying true to yourself and builds confidence in your choices.

It's important to remember that balancing expectations does not mean completely disregarding what others want or expect from you. It's about finding a healthy middle ground where you can remain true to yourself while considering others' perspectives.

Reflective Questions:

- How do the expectations of others affect my decision-making?
- What are my non-negotiable values that I won't compromise on?
- How can I communicate my needs more effectively to those around me?
- Maintaining Your Authenticity

Always align your actions with your core values and beliefs in your journey to manage expectations. This alignment ensures that your choices contribute to your sense of self rather than detracting from it. Remember, at the end of the day, you are the one who lives with your choices, so make them count for you.

Embracing Vulnerability: Discovering Strength in Openness

Vulnerability is often misunderstood as a weakness, but it is truly a source of strength. In this section, we'll explore what vulnerability really means, the situations in which it manifests, and how embracing it can enhance your journey toward self-love.

What is Vulnerability?

Vulnerability is the emotional state of being open to experiences, thoughts, and emotions that can lead to perceived risks such as emotional exposure or pain. It's about being honest with yourself and others about your feelings, desires, and fears.

Common Situations of Vulnerability

- **Expressing Emotions:** Revealing true feelings to others, such as telling someone you love them or expressing grief.

- **Trying New Things:** Putting yourself in situations where you might fail, like starting a new business or learning a new skill.

- **Asking for Help:** Admit you can't do something on your own and seek assistance from others.

- **Sharing Personal Stories:** Discuss personal experiences or challenges you might typically keep private.

- **Setting Boundaries:** Declaring your limits and asking others to respect them.

Strategies for Embracing Vulnerability

1. Recognize the Benefits:
Understand that vulnerability can lead to growth, stronger relationships, and increased self-awareness. Acknowledging the benefits can make it easier to embrace vulnerability as a positive and essential part of life.

2. Start Small:
Begin with small steps. Share something personal with a trusted friend, or express a minor concern at work. Gradually increase your comfort level by being open.

3. Practice Self-Compassion:
Be kind to yourself when you feel vulnerable. Recognize that feeling vulnerable is a universal human experience and nothing to be ashamed of.

4. Prepare for Various Outcomes:
While being open can lead to positive experiences, preparing emotionally for things that may not go as planned is important. This preparation can make you more resilient.

5. Reflect on Past Experiences:
Think about times when being vulnerable led to a positive outcome. Reflecting on these can boost your confidence in showing vulnerability in the future.

6. Develop Emotional Awareness:
Cultivate an awareness of your emotions through practices like mindfulness or journaling. This can help you understand and articulate your feelings more clearly when you are vulnerable.

7. Seek Supportive Environments:
Surround yourself with people who respect and support your openness. A supportive community can make it easier to practice vulnerability.

Encouraging Questions to Foster Vulnerability

- What am I afraid to tell someone because I fear their reaction?
- When have I felt most connected with others, and what made those moments special?
- How can I show up more authentically in my relationships and interactions?

Embracing vulnerability means seizing the opportunity to grow and deepen your connections with others. It allows us to be fully seen and authentic and build relationships based on trust and honesty. Practicing vulnerability reinforces your capacity for self-love, showing that you are worthy of being known, seen, and loved—just as you are.

Chapter 10: Living a Life Fueled by Self-Love

"Act as if what you do makes a difference. It does." – William James.

As you journey through life, the principle of self-love can illuminate your path and guide your decisions. When your choices are fueled by genuine self-love, you enhance your life and contribute positively to the world around you.

Making Self-Love-Driven Decisions

Self-love in decision-making involves prioritizing your needs, desires, and well-being. It's about choosing options that nurture your growth, protect your emotional energy, and promote your happiness and health.

Steps to Make Self-Love-Driven Decisions

1. Check in With Your Feelings:
Before making a decision, take a moment to assess how each option makes you feel. Does it cause stress or anxiety? Does it excite and energize you? Your emotions can be powerful indicators of what truly serves you.

2. Evaluate the Alignment with Your Values:
Ensure that your choices align with your core values. If integrity, honesty, or kindness are important to you, consider how your decisions reflect these values.

3. Consider the Long-Term Impact:
Think about how your decision will affect your future self. Will this choice lead you closer to where you want to be in life? Does it contribute to your long-term happiness and well-being?

4. Seek Advice, But Make Your Own Choice:
While seeking advice from trusted individuals is beneficial, ensure that the final decision resonates personally. You know yourself best and ultimately live with your choices.

5. Practice Saying No:
Making self-love-driven decisions involves declining opportunities and requests that don't align with your best interests. Remember, saying no to something that isn't right for you means saying yes to what is.

Start small by applying these strategies to everyday decisions. Reflect on each choice with the perspective of self-love. Did the decision contribute to your well-being? Did it reflect your values? Over time, this practice will become more natural, profoundly affecting your life's trajectory.

Extending Love to the Community: Enhancing Well-being Through Shared Compassion

Self-love doesn't end with the individual; it has a ripple effect that extends into the wider community. When you nurture love within yourself, you are more capable of spreading that love outward, contributing positively to the well-being of those around you.

How to Share Love in the Community

1. Volunteer Your Time:
Volunteering is a direct way to contribute positively to your community. Whether helping at a local food bank, tutoring students, or participating in community clean-ups, giving your time can significantly impact you.

2. Support Local Businesses:
Show love for your community by supporting local enterprises. Shop at local markets, eat at local restaurants and patronize local artisans. This not only helps sustain the local economy but also builds community ties.

3. Participate in Local Events:
Engage with your community by attending or organizing local events. Whether it's a charity run, a town fair, or a cultural festival, participation helps strengthen community bonds and fosters a sense of collective identity.

4. Advocate for Community Causes:
Become an advocate for issues that affect your community. This could involve campaigning for better local services, supporting community-led initiatives, or working on environmental conservation efforts.

5. Create Community Spaces:
Help develop spaces where the community can unite, such as gardens, parks, or art installations. These spaces provide a focal point for community interaction and shared activities.

Benefits of Community Engagement

Enhanced Social Networks:
Engaging in community activities expands your social network and can lead to meaningful relationships based on mutual interests and shared experiences.

Increased Personal Fulfillment:
Contributing to the community can provide a sense of purpose and fulfillment, enhancing your own well-being while helping others.

Improved Mental Health:
Community involvement has been linked to lower levels of stress and depression and higher feelings of happiness.

Real-Life Examples

Community Gardening:
Imagine participating in a community garden project. You contribute to creating a beautiful, shared space, connecting with neighbors, learning new skills, and enjoying the mental health benefits of gardening.

Local Mentorship Programs:
Consider volunteering as a mentor in local youth programs. This can be incredibly rewarding as you help

guide young people, witness their growth, and make a lasting impact on their lives.

Incorporate a mindset of community love into your daily life by looking for small ways to contribute and show care. Whether it's helping a neighbor, offering a kind word to a stranger, or organizing community activities, every act of love contributes to building a stronger, more resilient community.

By extending love beyond yourself and into your community, you enrich your life and create a more compassionate and connected world. Remember, the love you give is often the love you receive—multiplied.

Remember, self-love is not a destination; it's a journey that continues throughout your life. It evolves, grows, and deepens as you do.

Postpartum Depression and Self-Love

Navigating the challenges of postpartum depression can be overwhelming, but nurturing self-love during this time is essential for your well-being. Postpartum depression affects many new mothers, and it's important to acknowledge that what you're experiencing is not a reflection of your worth or abilities as a mother.

What is Postpartum Depression?

Postpartum depression is a mood disorder that affects women after childbirth. It is more intense and lasts longer than the "baby blues" many new mothers experience. While the baby blues typically begin a few days after birth and can last for up to two weeks, postpartum depression can start any time within the first year after childbirth and may persist for months if untreated.

Types and Symptoms of Postpartum Depression

- **Postpartum Depression:** This type is characterized by severe mood swings, excessive crying, difficulty bonding with your baby, withdrawal from family and friends, and overwhelming fatigue or loss of energy. You might also experience feelings of worthlessness, guilt, and anxiety.

- **Postpartum Anxiety:** This includes intense anxiety and constant worry that interfere with your ability to care for your baby or yourself. Symptoms may include panic attacks, shortness of breath, chest pain, dizziness, and constant fear that something terrible will happen.

- **Postpartum Obsessive-Compulsive Disorder (OCD):** This is marked by repetitive, intrusive thoughts and compulsions. For instance, you might have disturbing thoughts about harming your baby and engage in behaviors to reduce these fears, such as repeatedly checking on your baby.

- **Postpartum Psychosis:** This is a rare but severe form of postpartum depression that includes hallucinations, delusions, paranoia, and severe mood swings. It requires immediate medical attention as it can pose serious risks to both the mother and the baby.

Signs and Features to Look Out For

Recognizing the signs of postpartum depression is crucial for seeking timely help. Common symptoms include:

- Persistent sadness or low mood
- Loss of interest in activities you once enjoyed
- Changes in appetite and weight
- Difficulty sleeping or sleeping too much
- Intense irritability or anger
- Feelings of hopelessness, worthlessness, or guilt
- Difficulty concentrating or making decisions
- Severe anxiety or panic attacks
- Thoughts of harming yourself or your baby

Typically, women may start experiencing postpartum depression within the first few weeks after childbirth, but it can also begin later, up to a year postpartum. If you notice any of these symptoms persisting for more than two weeks, it's important to seek help.

Practical Strategies to Assist You

1. Acknowledge Your Feelings
First and foremost, allow yourself to feel what you're feeling without judgment. It's okay to feel sad, anxious, or overwhelmed. Recognize that these emotions are valid and part of your journey. By acknowledging your feelings, you begin the process of understanding and healing.

2. Seek Professional Help
Don't hesitate to reach out to healthcare professionals for support. A therapist or counselor specializing in postpartum depression can provide valuable guidance and coping strategies. Additionally, discussing your symptoms with your doctor can help you find appropriate treatments, such as therapy or medication.

3. Build a Support Network
Surround yourself with supportive friends and family who understand what you're going through. Join support groups, either in person or online, where you can share your experiences and hear from others who have faced similar challenges. Having a community can provide comfort and reduce feelings of isolation.

4. Practice Self-Compassion
Be kind to yourself during this time. Understand that it's okay to not have everything under control. Speak to yourself with the same compassion you would offer a close friend. Remind yourself that you are doing your best and that asking for help is okay.

5. Set Realistic Expectations
Adjust your expectations and be gentle with yourself. You don't have to be the perfect mother,

partner, or person. Focus on small, manageable tasks each day and celebrate your accomplishments, no matter how minor they may seem. This approach can help reduce feelings of overwhelm and boost your confidence.

6. Prioritize Self-Care
Make time for activities that nurture your mind and body. Self-care is crucial, whether it's taking a warm bath, going for a walk, or simply taking a few minutes to breathe deeply. Schedule these activities into your day, even if it's just for a short period.

7. Connect with Your Baby
Spend quiet moments bonding with your baby. Skin-to-skin contact, gentle rocking, and talking to your baby can strengthen your emotional connection. These intimate moments can help foster a sense of closeness and well-being.

8. Use Mindfulness Techniques
Incorporate mindfulness practices into your daily routine to help manage stress and anxiety. Techniques such as deep breathing, meditation, or mindful walking can bring you back to the present moment and reduce negative thoughts.

9. Nourish Your Body
Focus on eating nutritious foods that give you energy and make you feel good. Proper nutrition can significantly impact your mood and energy levels. Stay hydrated, and try to include a variety of fruits, vegetables, lean proteins, and whole grains in your diet.

10. Celebrate Small Victories
Acknowledge and celebrate small victories each day. Whether managing to shower, preparing a meal, or spending quality time with your baby,

recognizing these achievements can help build a positive mindset and reinforce self-love.

Remember, postpartum depression is a temporary condition, and with the right support and strategies, you can overcome it. Be patient with yourself, seek help when needed, and practice self-love every day. You deserve care, kindness, and compassion, both from others and yourself.

Conclusion

Reflecting on this journey of self-love, I am overwhelmed by the transformation that has unfolded in my life. From the shadows of a constrained existence to the radiant light of autonomy and self-compassion, my path has been both arduous and enlightening. Sharing my story with you isn't just about recounting past events; it's about revealing the profound impact that embracing self-love can have on one's life. My journey has taught me that self-love is not merely a state of feeling good about oneself but a powerful practice of continually choosing to believe in one's own worth, even in the face of life's inevitable challenges.

As you reflect on your own journey through these pages, remember that self-love is an ever-evolving process. It's not about reaching a destination where you are perfect and complete, but rather about embracing the journey itself, with all its ups and downs. Each day presents a new opportunity to show kindness, forgive yourself for your faults, and nurture your aspirations. I encourage you to carry forward the practices and insights you've gained, allowing them to light your way through dark times and enhance your joy in the good times. Self-love is your secret weapon, protector, and guide—it is the key to unlocking your fullest potential.

The impact of self-love extends far beyond the individual. It influences every interaction you have and every decision you make. By choosing self-love, you improve your life and contribute to a kinder, more compassionate world. Imagine a world where everyone acts out of love and respect for themselves and each other. The ripple effects of this could be revolutionary. This isn't just an idle dream; it starts with you, right here, right now. Your commitment to self-love creates a better world for yourself and those around you.

Looking to the future, let this book remind you that your self-love journey is continuous. There will be days when self-love feels natural and easy and other days when it requires conscious effort.

Keep pushing forward, keep striving for growth, and let every challenge be a stepping stone to greater self-understanding and acceptance. Remember, you are worth this effort.

And finally, as you move forward, share the message of self-love. Talk about your journey, support others in theirs, and create a community where love and acceptance are the foundations. Your story could be the beacon that guides someone else out of their darkest hour. Let us spread this message far and wide, fostering a culture where self-love is revered and practiced universally.

If this book has touched your life, helped you see things in a new light, or inspired you to start your own journey of self-love, I humbly ask you to **"leave a positive review"** on Amazon. Your support not only helps me but also helps others discover the transformative power of self-love. Together, let's continue to build a community that cherishes and promotes self-love, creating a legacy that will inspire generations to come.

© Jenifer Taylor

Connect with the Author

Thank you for joining me on this journey. If you'd like to connect, share your story, or seek further guidance, please visit my website at www.counsellingsupportservice.com. I look forward to hearing from you!

REFRENCES

https://www.mettapsych.com/selfdefeating-behaviors-adults#:~:text=Self%2Ddefeating%20behaviors%20are%20behaviors,exhausted%20and%20bad%20about%20ourselves.
https://psychcentral.com/health/help-your-clients-stop-self-defeating-behaviors
https://www.youtube.com/watch?v=TYiaSbi-XzY
https://www.betterup.com/blog/self-love
https://www.healthline.com/health/13-self-love-habits-every-woman-needs-to-have
https://www.ncbi.nlm.nih.gov/pmc/articles/PMC2790748/#:~:text=Research%20indicates%20that%20self%2Dcompassion,rumination%20and%20fear%20of%20failure.
https://www.calendar.com/blog/cultivating-your-authentic-self-a-journey-of-self-discovery-and-fulfillment/
https://medium.com/hello-love/three-popular-myths-about-self-love-c79825b14c3a
https://sarahsteckler.com/blog/the-biggest-myths-of-self-love-debunked
https://nesslabs.com/self-love
https://medium.com/echoes-of-discovery/the-psychology-of-self-love-building-confidence-from-within-025fe53571e2
https://medium.com/hello-love/three-popular-myths-about-self-love-c79825b14c3a
https://esoftskills.com/the-role-of-self-love-in-personal-development/
https://www.samvednacare.com/blog/importance-of-self-love-in-improving-your-mental-health/
https://www.calm.com/blog/negative-self-talk
https://www.verywellmind.com/negative-self-talk-and-how-it-affects-us-4161304
https://www.gaucherdisease.org/blog/5-exercises-for-building-emotional-resilience/?gad_source=1&gclid=CjwKCAjwmYCzBhA6Ei

wAxFwfgIVdpAt9qStJv3xhjQfxx4O3oBUStcwky976PY8FO
o4HbAU-vlup8xoCRQcQAvD_BwE
https://warwick.ac.uk/services/wss/topics/emotional_resilience/
https://www.linkedin.com/pulse/why-self-love-key-happier-fulfilling-life-tanvi-vyas
https://simipsychologicalgroup.com/5-critical-reasons-self-love-is-necessary-for-happiness/
https://insightbhllc.com/4-ways-to-begin-loving-yourself-after-childhood-abuse/#:~:text=Healing%20from%20childhood%20abuse%20and,and%20your%20sense%20of%20self.
https://silviaturon.com/how-to-love-yourself-after-surviving-childhood-trauma/
https://www.ncbi.nlm.nih.gov/pmc/articles/PMC6844133/
https://www.sciencedirect.com/science/article/pii/S1877042811027637
https://www.medicalnewstoday.com/articles/effects-of-childhood-trauma#healing
https://www.betterup.com/blog/childhood-trauma
https://positivepsychology.com/reparenting/#:~:text=Engaging%20in%20reparenting%20practices%20cultivates,love%20(Schwartz%2C%202021).
https://www.bigselfschool.com/post/inner-child-work
https://medium.com/crows-feet/letting-go-and-choosing-forgiveness-as-an-act-of-self-love-6f18b9949a92
https://balanceapp.com/blog/self-forgiveness-guide-to-letting-go
https://suntiasmith.com/2016/02/02/art-of-letting-go-forgiveness/
https://www.heretohelp.bc.ca/infosheet/body-image-self-esteem-and-mental-health#:~:text=If%20you%20don't%20like,body%20the%20respect%20it%20deserves.
https://www.innerbody.com/relationship-between-body-image-and-self-esteem
https://www.ncbi.nlm.nih.gov/pmc/articles/PMC8249135/

https://www.verywellmind.com/what-is-body-positivity-4773402#:~:text=Body%20positivity%20refers%20to%20the,good%20about%20how%20it%20looks.
https://health.clevelandclinic.org/body-positivity-vs-body-neutrality
https://theendlessspiral.com/2023/07/03/embracing-self-acceptance-a-journey-to-love-and-appreciate-your-body/
https://www.blueridgetreatment.com/post/overcome-a-negative-body-image
https://tinybuddha.com/blog/strong-relationships-stem-self-love-develop/
https://balanceapp.com/blog/how-to-love-yourself-in-a-relationship
https://www.papyrus-uk.org/setting-boundaries/#:~:text=Some%20ways%20to%20set%20healthy,and%20seeking%20support%20when%20needed.
https://positivepsychology.com/great-self-care-setting-healthy-boundaries/
https://medium.com/@enuska/breaking-the-cycle-embracing-freedom-from-toxic-relationships-05d93144521f
https://www.katiavlachos.com/blog/how-to-break-free-from-a-toxic-relationship
https://www.lifecoach.com/articles/relationships/building-connections-tips-for-cultivating-deeper-relationships/
https://www.fostercounseling.org/resources-and-blog/healthy-relationships-lasting-connection
https://www.few.org/2024/02/13/5-ways-to-overcome-self-love-challenges-to-foster-personal-career-growth/#:~:text=Self%2Dlove%20plays%20a%20significant,tremendous%20career%20success%20and%20fulfillment.
forbes.com/sites/bryanrobinson/2021/02/05/how-self-love-boosts-job-performance-and-career-success/
https://www.forbes.com/sites/forbescoachescouncil/2021/03/23/overcoming-imposter-syndrome-four-proven-methods-to-increase-your-confidence/?sh=6002da79755c
https://www.mindtools.com/azi07m7/impostor-syndrome

https://timesofindia.indiatimes.com/readersblog/happinesssanta/honoring-your-needs-the-liberation-of-saying-no-55957/
teyxo.com/lifestyle/how-saying-no-can-empower-your-life/
https://mpowerminds.com/blog/the-connection-between-work-life-balance-and-professional-growth-find-harmony-in-your-career-and-personal-life#:~:text=Tips%20for%20Finding%20Harmony%3A,negotiable%20part%20of%20your%20routine.
https://fierileadership.com/work-life-balance-finding-harmony-between-your-professional-and-personal-life/
https://www.mindtools.com/ax3c2aw/celebrating-achievement
https://medium.com/@joepardavila/recognizing-your-successes-a-journey-to-self-awareness-and-gratitude-6e114f3db329s
https://www.calm.com/blog/how-to-love-yourself
https://aeryliving.com/blogs/wellbeing-journal/5-ways-to-practice-self-love
https://innerspacecounselling.com.au/the-art-of-self-compassion-a-journey-to-mental-well-being-and-self-improvement/
https://www.counselling-directory.org.uk/memberarticles/whats-the-difference-between-mindfulness-and-self-compassion
https://mindfulmonkey.in/blogs/mindfulness/unlocking-inner-wisdom-the-importance-of-journaling-for-mindful-living
https://clarewalshcoaching.com/new-blog/unleashing-your-inner-wisdom-the-magic-of-journaling
https://beatanxiety.me/common-self-love-obstacles-people-face/#:~:text=If%20you%20are%20surrounded%20by,you%20feel%20positive%20about%20yourself.
https://www.marriage.com/advice/mental-health/self-love/
https://www.linkedin.com/pulse/embracing-vulnerability-key-unlocking-deeper-dan-stillman-hql3e

https://www.culture-principles.com/the-power-of-openness-lessons-in-vulnerability-and-inclusion/
https://pubmed.ncbi.nlm.nih.gov/9120033/
https://www.unicef.org/parenting/mental-health/what-postpartum-depression

Printed in Great Britain
by Amazon